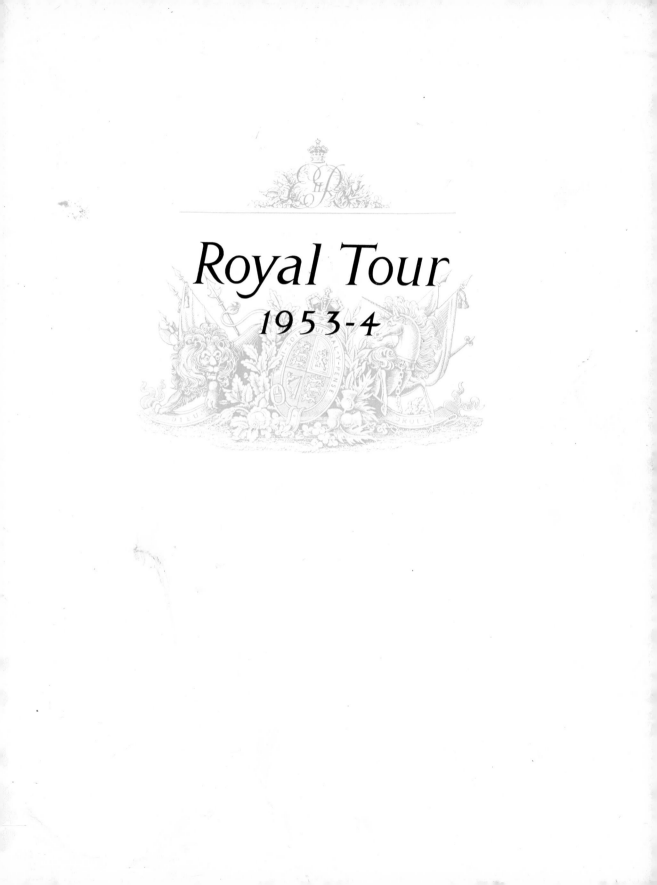

Royal Tour
1953-4

*Her Majesty the Queen and the Duke of Edinburgh
at the City of Melbourne Royal Ball*

Royal Tour

1953-4

WYNFORD
VAUGHAN
THOMAS

Hutchinson Stratford Place London

HUTCHINSON & CO. (PUBLISHERS) LTD

London   Melbourne   Sydney
Auckland   Bombay   Cape Town
New York   Toronto

Printed by
WILLIAM BRENDON & SON LTD
The Mayflower Press
Watford

*"Her Majesty's ship Gothic is more spacious
and travels faster than the Golden Hind, but it may well
be that the journey the Queen is about to take will be no less
auspicious and the treasure she brings back no less bright than
when Drake first sailed an English ship round the world."*

SIR WINSTON CHURCHILL

House of Commons   19th Nov. 1953

Departure
Nine o'clock
Monday
November 23rd
1953

Chapter One

BERMUDA JAMAICA FIJI TONGA

NINE O'CLOCK, MONDAY, NOVEMBER 23rd, 1953. A moment of deep significance in the ancient and honourable history of our Royal House. It was then that the gleaming, silvery-white Stratocruiser, *Canopus*, roared down the long runway of London Airport, and lifted into the grey night sky over the capital, carrying Her Majesty the Queen and the Duke of Edinburgh westward on the first stage of their historic six-months' journey around the world and the Commonwealth. London had given the royal ambassadors an emotional and deeply felt farewell. Thousands had gathered along the fifteen-mile route from Buckingham Palace to the airport. Again and again the crowd had surged on to the roadway and Her Majesty had ordered that her car should travel slowly so that she could wave her thanks for the cheering and the shouts of *"Bon Voyage"*. At the airport, Sir Winston Churchill and the High Commissioners of the Dominions that Her Majesty was to visit, conveyed their official good wishes for the success of the tour. The Queen Mother and Princess Margaret said their "good-bye" inside the aircraft itself. Then the Queen and the Duke came to the doorway of *Canopus*. Millions who watched on their television sets all over Britain saw them give a final

wave. The doors closed and the four powerful engines of the Stratocruiser leapt into life. There was no delay. The aircraft taxied into position, and in a matter of minutes *Canopus* was airborne and away, its twin lights making two swiftly moving and hopeful stars across the vast night sky over London.

There was no one who looked up and saw it go high overhead who didn't wave and wish 'God speed' to the royal travellers, for they were starting on a voyage unique even in the annals of our much-travelled royal family. This was to be the longest tour ever undertaken by a reigning monarch, a wonderful demonstration of the strength of the bonds that hold our Commonwealth together. When he spoke in the House of Commons on the eve of the Queen's departure, Sir Winston Churchill, with his unrivalled felicity of phrase, had compared Her Majesty's journey to Sir Francis Drake's voyage round the world. He prophesied that she would bring back a treasure no less bright— the love and loyalty of her subjects over- seas.

So, swiftly, out of the November cold of Britain the Queen flew towards the sun- shine and the warmth of the welcome that awaited her. Her first stop gave her an indication of the enthusiasm and excite- ment that would accompany her wherever she went in the six months ahead. *Canopus*

The Queen Mother and Princess Margaret wave 'God speed'

had made the flight across the Atlantic in just under ten hours and had put down at Gander in Newfoundland at 3.23 in the morning by local time. According to the official schedule the Queen was to sleep undisturbed, while the aircraft was refuelled. But a crowd had been waiting all night in the hope of catching a glimpse of her. They sang 'For she's a jolly good fellow' with such right good will that the Queen and the Duke quickly gave up all ideas of sleeping. They dressed hurriedly and came to the door. They had warm handshakes for two of the Mounties whom they recognized from their 1951 tour, and the Queen smiled: "It's nice to be in Canada again, even if only for a short stay." The crowd cheered and shouted "Have a good trip. Come back and see us again."

Canada's welcome had been unofficial. Now ahead of the Queen was the first official ceremony of the tour, her visit to Bermuda.

For weeks this small but enchanting island, that is almost lost in the Atlantic, had been in the throes of frenzied preparation. Every house seemed to have been repainted until they all shone a dazzling white. Triumphal arches spanned the roads in every parish and there had been fierce competition for the best. The winner, by universal consent, was the Parish of Pembroke. Here the inhabitants had dredged the sea for an astonishing variety of sea shells to decorate their arch and volunteer divers had worked until the last minute before the Queen arrived, hunting for still rarer and more colourful shells. The local Calypso singers rose to new heights of inspiration with a Calypso which began:

"Flags is flying, boots is shined,
Only hope de weather keep fine."

and ended with the rousing and loyal chorus:

"Welcome to our Gracious Queen,
Who we have loved but never seen."

Arrival at Bermuda, the first official stop

After addressing the Colonial Parliament of Bermuda, Her Majesty and the Duke of Edinburgh are cheered by the happy islanders

The weather may not have been quite as fine as the Calypsonians hoped, but it was bright enough and warm when, punctually at 10 a.m. on 24th November, the royal aircraft touched down on Bermuda's big airfield, that was carved out of the coral rock during the war. She was met by the Governor, Lieut.-General Sir Alexander Hood, and received a most dignified official welcome. She drove through every parish and town in the island. She visited the ancient church of St. Peter's in the old capital of Bermuda, St. George's, and she received an address of welcome at the Sessions House in the present capital, Hamilton. Here she took her seat on the Speaker's Chair in the oldest Commonwealth Parliament outside Westminster. Bermuda lives by her American tourist trade, but the island is fiercely proud of her ties with the Crown. The House of Assembly gave Her Majesty an overwhelming reception.

But splendid though these official ceremonies were, I think that both the Queen and her Bermudian subjects will remember best the unofficial and unusual incidents that accompanied the royal tour of the island. For example, there was the car in which the Queen and the Duke rode from the airport. Her Majesty must have rubbed her eyes with surprise when she saw it. It was a 14 h.p. convertible, which was just about large enough for the Queen to squeeze into beside the Duke. For years Bermuda has been the last stronghold of the horse, and the ban on cars was only withdrawn in 1946. Even now all cars over 14 h.p. are illegal. So Her Majesty gladly obeyed Bermudian law and drove

A Royal drive through Bermuda

smiling into the hearts of all who saw her in the smallest car ever used in a royal procession.

The royal yacht in which the Queen made her afternoon trip over the clear waters of the Great Sound was equally surprising and delightful. It was simply the gallant old ferry-boat, *Wilhelmina*, glorified and repainted for the occasion. And her pilot, Mr. R. C. Reginald Dill, must surely be the proudest man in Bermuda. The Queen gave him the Royal Victorian Medal, a decoration which is in the personal gift of the sovereign, and Mr. Dill declares that he will never take it off, no matter what he wears or what he does in the future.

Like Mr. Dill, Bermuda will never discard the charm and delight of the Royal visit. There were tears in the eyes of many in the great crowd that assembled at the early hour of six o'clock on 25th November, to see the royal airliner leave from Kindley Field. A lone piper sounded the 'Road to the Isles'. Then *Canopus* took off, and headed south, carrying Her Majesty over the seas to isles as romantic and as loyal as those celebrated in the piper's song— the islands of the West Indies.

To Jamaica fell the honour of receiving

Reviewing the Guard of Honour at Montego Bay Airport, Jamaica

the Queen in her West Indian possessions, and Jamaica carried out its loyal duty with true Caribbean gusto. The plane touched down just before ten o'clock in the morning at Montego Bay, the holiday resort in the north-west corner of the island, and the happy, unsophisticated cries of 'She's beautiful' that came clear over the cheers from the waiting crowd indicated straight away that Jamaica's welcome was going to be no formal affair. It turned out to be as joyous and colourful as a Calypso. First came the royal progress right through the heart of the island to the capital, Kingston —120 miles of enchantment in which Jamaica outdid anything imagined by Hollywood and the travel agencies. The road ran alongside an ocean of vivid blue, that foamed in dazzling white rollers on to palm-shaded coral beaches. Triumphal arches spanned the winding highway. Every little town and village *en route* was packed with people whose dresses were as brilliant as their smiles of welcome. The Queen and the Duke defied the fierce

tropical sun and rode in an open limousine, and behind them came the Governor, Sir Hugh Foot, and the smiling, grey-haired handsome Chief Minister, Mr. Bustamante.

The cavalcade stopped for lunch at Silver Sands, the sort of place you dream about on a foggy, winter's day in London. The Queen and the Duke went for a swim in a lukewarm sea, and the menu for lunch had the right Jamaican flavour with roast sucking pig, black crab, roasted breadfruit and yams.

The rain that caught them high up in the mountains after lunch was equally Jamaican. It cascaded down in a flamboyant, tropical downpour. At last, after a day that began for the Queen at 4.30 in the morning in far-off Bermuda, she reached King's House in Kingston, her temporary home in Jamaica.

The Queen and the Duke might have been pardoned if they had taken it easy after the excitement of their arrival, and, officially, the programme for Thursday was described as a light one. But a royal tour is remorseless in its demands on the stamina of the central figures. The royal couple were out at 8 a.m. to inspect military and naval units stationed in the Caribbean. Then came a rapturous welcome from 20,000 school children at Sabina Park, followed by a quick stop to plant the first of the 'salute of a million trees', with which Jamaica is combating erosion and celebrating the royal visit. Then on to the Legislature, where Her Majesty, from the Speaker's Chair, gave a message of importance for the political future of the West Indies. She concluded:

"May you build on the principles of Parliamentary Government which have been tested and tried over the centuries and found to be sure and true, and may your efforts to serve those whom you represent be crowned with success."

All through the warm afternoon, Her Majesty had informal talks with leading representatives of the educational world in Jamaica, while outside the grounds of King's House, the sprawling, gaily decorated capital was filled with excited crowds, singing, dancing and celebrating. All the natural gaiety of Kingston was released on this second day of the royal visit by the very presence of their Queen in the midst of a laughter-loving, joyous people.

The celebrations were still in full swing at midnight when 3,000 guests crowded the lawns of King's House for the official reception. The Queen and the Duke looked down from the balcony as a team of gaily dressed folk singers put their hearts into an unrestrained rendering of 'Good evening, Mistress Flanagan, how are you this evening?' Every loyal Jamaican could join

in the chorus of this song, and reply— 'Never better!' For this was a day that the whole of the West Indies would remember with pride and joy for many days to come.

Jamaica retained its reputation for doing the delightfully unexpected with gusto to the very last moment of the royal visit. The Queen began the final day of her visit with an investiture, which was the first in history to be held outside Britain. She made a tour of the new University College of the West Indies, and then drove with the Duke to historic Port Royal, the ancient fortress which lies far out on the other side of the wide lagoon of Kingston Harbour. Here Sir Henry Morgan had held sway, and Nelson had paced the battlements, watching in vain for the French fleet. It was here, too, that Jamaica staged its unofficial farewell gesture.

As Her Majesty walked to the landing stage to go on board the liner *Gothic*, which lay anchored in the bay, a Mr. Kidd slipped past the guards. He was an ordinary Jamaican citizen fired by an extraordinary idea. With old-world courtesy he placed his coat before the Queen for her to walk on, and thus became the first Sir Walter Raleigh of the tour! It didn't matter that the police misunderstood and hustled the romantically minded Mr. Kidd hurriedly off the scene. The rest of the West Indies, and Britain too, laughed and applauded. Jamaica had welcomed the Queen with a charming and heart-warming informality.

With regret Her Majesty watched her loyal islands of the Caribbean fade astern. For the next few weeks the Shaw-Savill liner, *Gothic*, was the moving centre of the royal tour. As she sailed out of Kingston

*(i) Her Majesty shakes hands with the Speaker of the Legislature (ii) bestows the Order of Commander of the British Empire on Colonel A. G. Curphey during an investiture and
(iii) discusses the welfare of the patients at the University Hospital with Nursing Sister Francis*

Reviewing Jamaican school children on the famous Sabina Park Cricket Ground

Dining with the Governor, Sir Hugh Foot

Being entertained by native musicians

"Good-bye Jamaica, and thank you"

harbour she looked perfect for her role of 'royal yacht'. Her hull and her super-structure were painted a gleaming white, and her commander, Captain David Aitchison, together with his crew, were rightly proud of the way that the ship had been overhauled from stem to stern to make her a true home for the Queen. Her Majesty and the Duke had their quarters aft on the Boat Deck. Here they could re-lax and enjoy themselves for a brief moment free from the iron discipline of etiquette that inevitably surrounds the public ap-pearances of royalty. An illuminated map in the vestibule showed the route of the voyage, and the position of the ship was marked on it by moving pin-points of light. *Gothic* also had its own cinema and a special transmitter for the use of the press and radio men on board.

Life passed pleasantly as the ship slipped steadily southward through calm, blue seas. There was one exotic interlude at the Panama Canal, when the little tropical republic of Panama put its whole heart into a royal welcome that was completely Latin in its unrestrained pleasure. It was a day of sunshine and speechmaking, of cheers and laughter, with the Queen and the Duke driving the length of the Canal through wildly excited crowds. It ended, as all tropic days should end, with a splen-didly staged banquet and cabaret under the brightly sparkling stars.

Over a Pacific Ocean that lived up to its name, the royal liner now steamed south-ward towards the enchanted islands of Fiji and Tonga. Calm seas, clear skies, and warm weather were the order of the day as the *Gothic* crossed the Equator, while, ahead

of her, Fiji prepared to go wild with excite-ment.

Her Majesty has no more loyal subjects than the native Fijians. On the big-scale maps their country may look a mere dot on the face of the ocean but the Colony of Fiji is, in reality, a string of islands, some of them large and mountainous and others small, palm fringed and circled by gleaming coral reefs. London will remember with affection the Fijians marching in the Coro-nation procession—men of magnificent physique with fine mops of wiry hair who wore the distinctive shark-toothed skirt of the islands, the sulu. Their capital, Suva, lies on the largest of the islands, Viti Levu, and as the *Gothic* sailed into the harbour through the gap in the reef on that memorable morning of 17th December the city looked its lovely best against its background of green, forest-clad moun-tains.

Twenty outrigger canoes which had sailed 200 miles from the outlying islands, escorted the royal liner to her anchorage, and the guns thundered as the Governor, Sir Ronald Garvey, accompanied by Lady Garvey, came on board to greet Her Majesty.

But Fiji is a land where tradition is still closely observed and before the Queen could go on shore the leading chiefs were also invited to board the *Gothic* to perform the age-old ceremony of the 'Cavuikelekele' or the formal invitation to land. In brilliant hot sunshine the Queen sat under an awning on the upper deck and Ratu Tevita Ululakega, paramount chief of Lau, came forward on his knees and presented the Queen with a 'Tambua', a whale's tooth

The Queen photographing her husband
enjoying himself while participating in the
'Crossing the line' ceremony

*The Queen steps ashore at Fiji.
Bedecked with flags the Gothic can be
seen in the background*

which is the most prized possession of any Fijian ruler. It was a mark of undying friendship and established an immediate bond between the Queen and her Fijian people.

Suva was now ready to receive the Queen, on a day on which everything went right. Little three-year-old Mei, daughter of the second in command of the Fijian battalion in Malaya, won the Queen's heart as she came forward like a tiny, exquisite doll and presented a bouquet as big as herself. Mei bowed and then clapped her hands three times as dictated by Fijian custom. "How lovely!" the Queen murmured in admiration.

Her Majesty in turn won the hearts of thousands of excited Fijians who had packed the streets and crowded into Albert Park when she drank the ceremonial cup of yangona, or 'kava' as it is called throughout the Pacific.

The drink was prepared with elaborate ceremonial from pounded roots and was presented to the Queen in a coco-nut bowl as a symbol of welcome. "Vinaka" was the verdict of the Fijian chiefs, meaning "very good indeed".

Then followed the lovely Fijian dances with long lines of men and women in their brightly coloured costumes garlanded with flowers, who swayed to the languorous rhythm of the 'lakalaka', and the establishment of a new tradition in Fiji. No longer will the islanders stand in respectful quiet before their rulers. They now cheer with wild, unrestrained enthusiasm.

For it was a day which the people of Suva will never forget. Long will they talk of the Queen's deep interest in the

A little Fijian girl proudly presents her bouquet

progress of medicine when she saw the new Central Medical School, and of her delight in the singing of the girls of the Adi Cakobau School. Above all they will remember her smiling grace as she drove to attend the state ball at the Grand Pacific Hotel. Torchbearers ran alongside the royal car forming a line of leaping, moving flame through the city, and fireworks sparkled amongst the stars when at last Her Majesty left the ballroom and came out on to the balcony. She wore a full state dress of silver blue lace over blue tulle graced with the order of the Garter, and the diamond tiara which she inherited from her beloved grandmother Queen Mary.

For twenty minutes she stood with the Duke of Edinburgh while the thousands who waited below in the darkness sang and cheered. This will always be Fiji's own special picture of the Queen—a slim, smiling figure, regal yet full of the charm of youth—set against the warm beauty of the tropic night.

Suva is the capital of Fiji, but on the western side of Viti Levu lie the great sugar plantations on which so much of Fiji's prosperity depends. Here Fiji and India join hands for the plantations are worked by thousands of Indians who have now been settled in the Colony for three generations.

On Friday morning 20,000 people swarmed into the streets of the little town of Lautoka as the flying boat bringing Her Majesty from Suva made a perfect landing in the harbour. She drove to the sports meeting through streets which had been transformed into a paradise of flowers.

The royal car drove for miles under flower-laden arches and past baskets of crimson flamboyants that were as gay as the saris worn by the Indian ladies.

The proudest man in the welcome was eighty-three-year-old Gulab Khan. He had served with Lord Roberts in the Sudan and he stood firm and upright in spite of his age, in the ranks of the guard of honour.

The most exciting moment of the day occurred after the sports meeting ended, when the crowd broke the barriers and the royal car almost disappeared in the middle of thousands of flag-waving, cheering Indians and Fijians, who surely got the closest and most unorthodox view of royalty that anyone obtained on the whole tour.

At last the smiling and delighted royal visitors were rescued and driven for a well-earned rest to the Governor's 'Bure'— the thatched-roofed chief's house on the hills above Lautoka. Here, guarded by her Fijian warriors and served with Fijian food that included prawns cooked in coco-nut milk and fish roasted on embers and served in a wrapping of banana leaves, the Queen and the Duke took a last look over the rich, tropical landscape. "It's been a lovely day," was Her Majesty's comment.

But it was not only Lautoka that deserved the praise of the Queen. The whole of the

Her Majesty leans back fascinated by the dancing warriors of Fiji

Fiji visit had a quality of warm-hearted enthusiasm which was linked to ancient ceremony and present-day grace and charm.

When the flying boat *Aotearoa II* took the Queen and the Duke eastwards from Suva towards the next stage of their tour there was deep affection mingled with the sadness of parting in the voices of Her Majesty's Fijian subjects as they sang the haunting farewell song of the islands, 'Isa Lei'.

Giant Fiji guards of honour appear to dwarf their dainty monarch

The famous traditional Spear Dance

An indian chief offers gifts to the Queen aboard the liner Gothic

Queen Salote says "Welcome to Tonga"

The royal party advance, and the women sit to indicate respect

Away to the west of Fiji lie the islands of the Tongan group, the Friendly Islands as Captain Cook called them. They have now been placed firmly on the map by the magic of a Queen's smile. Tonga is an independent kingdom under British protection with a long and colourful story, but the most important event in her recent history was surely that Coronation Day in far-off London when Queen Salote rode through the rain into the hearts of the British people.

All Tonga determined that when Queen Elizabeth came to the Friendly Islands she too would receive a welcome as warm-hearted as that given to Queen Salote by the folk of Britain.

The whole population of the scattered islands seemed to have crowded into the tiny capital of Nukualofa where the decorations had an imaginative grace which is the secret of the charm of Polynesia. Gay arches were everywhere through-

out the town. In one of them thirty-two small Tongan boys remained hidden in the foliage ready to thrust out Union Jacks and Tongan flags as the royal car passed underneath. Another bore the word 'Welcome' on one side and 'We Love You' on the other, while an enormous carpet of tapa cloth, the fabric of the islands, covered the whole length of the roadway leading to the War Memorial.

Queen Salote's palace was given over entirely to her royal guests. It is a charming Victorian building, with wide verandas, and a gay, pointed roof, with the royal chapel close at hand. The grounds go down to the sea under superb Norfolk Island pines and waving coconut palms. This is the South Seas at their most romantic and

TOP: *A Wesleyan Church minister greets the Queen*
CENTRE: *Inspecting the island's miniature army*
BOTTOM: *Laying a wreath on Tonga's war memorial*

picturesque. From the moment the Queen and the Duke went ashore to be welcomed by Queen Salote and her heir apparent, Prince Tungi, everything went with a swing. The Tongans were delighted with the charming contrast presented by the two Queens as they walked together— Queen Elizabeth, petite and smiling beside the tall and dignified figure of Queen Salote. But both of them seemed radiant with the pleasure of being together again. Then as a light rain started falling the two queens put up their umbrellas, looked at each other—and smiled broadly. Did their thoughts go back to rain that fell on Coronation Day in London?

But the Tongan rain didn't last long and there was warm sunshine for the climax of Nukualofa's first day of royal festival, the feast. This was no ordinary, formal meal. Rather was it a banquet on the ancient opulent scale of the South Seas, the sort of overflowing hospitality that the old Kings of Tonga offered to the early voyagers in the eighteenth century.

Graceful awnings of thatch had been built along the Mal'ae, the carefully tended green sward that stretches to the water's edge before the Royal Palace. Beneath them were placed mountains of Tongan food, pyramids of roast pig, and whole shiploads of yams, coconuts and fruit. It was a sight to gladden the heart of Gargantua. The guests fell upon it with a will, for Tongan appetites are on a royal scale. Seldom has so much been eaten by so

At the welcoming feast Queen Salote is a jovial hostess

many who left so little. For as soon as the official guests had retired from the gastronomic contest, the event was thrown open to the general public, and it is a matter of history that not a leg of pork or a yam remained untackled.

The feast was a glorious affair and so were the dances, when the maidens of Tonga, clad in bodices decorated with shells and skirts of tapa cloth, swayed to the slow, languorous rhythm of flute and drums. This was the Tonga of romance, an enchanted isle where all was warmth, music and joy.

How the Friendly Islands lived up to their name. Every Tongan did his or her best to make the Queen and the Duke feel that this was an informal holiday visit, a glorious picnic in the sun.

There were smiles and laughter everywhere, even when the lights failed, as Her Majesty and Queen Salote were about to sit down to their private dinner at the British Consulate. And there was still song and rejoicing far into the night, when, in accordance with ancient custom, fifty watch fires glowed in the grounds of the Royal Palace as the Tongan warriors guarded their royal guests.

At dawn on Sunday the soft, melodious sound of flutes serenaded the Queen, an unusual sound, for in Tonga, as in many places throughout the Pacific, the flute is blown with the nose.

Queen Salote walked with the Queen and the Duke in the royal gardens before the heat of the day, and introduced them to the oldest inhabitant of Tonga, the famous tortoise Tui Malila, which was reputed to have been brought to the island by Captain Cook himself.

The royal party then drove to attend the service at Tonga's new and impressive Methodist Church where they were deeply moved by the singing of the huge congregation. Here was another side of the Friendly Islands. The Queen and her people are sincerely religious and Sunday on Tonga is a day set firmly apart from the rest of the week.

But there is no suggestion of gloom about the simple religious faith of Tonga. Laughter and gaiety ruled at the picnic held on the Queen's country estate.

At last came the moment of farewell. The royal cars were decorated with streamers of greenery and flowers. Slowly they drove through the cheering crowds to the wharf. A garland of flowers had been placed around the Queen's neck by Princess Mata aho, and the Duke and the members of the royal staff were also garlanded with the traditional 'Leis'. There was more than a hint of tears and sadness in Queen Salote's warm-hearted smile as she stood waving her white handkerchief while the *Gothic*, with her guests at the saluting base on the upper deck, pulled slowly away from the hospitable shores of Tonga. In the wake of the *Gothic* the garlands of flowers were cast upon the waters, as commanded by ancient custom. The Queen of Tonga sent her last message to the Queen of England. 'Ofatu—Good Luck.'

*This colourful scene is at Albert Park, Fiji, where the Royal
party, led by the Governor, Sir Roland Garvie, proceeds past a Guard of Honour
of Fijian women in National dress who are sitting as a mark of respect*

Chapter Two

NEW ZEALAND

"YOUR Majesty will be left in no doubt of the deep loyalty and affection which the people of New Zealand bear towards you."

This was the message that Mr. Holland, the Prime Minister of New Zealand, gave the Queen on her arrival in the most distant of her dominions, and in the eventful weeks that followed, every single part of the country set out to prove the truth of Mr. Holland's words up to the very hilt.

Auckland set the example. How New Zealand's largest city longed for a day of sunshine in which to welcome the *Gothic* up the long reaches of its magnificent harbour! The luck of the weather provided rough water and grey skies, but not for a moment was Auckland dismayed. Its citizens remembered London on Coronation Day and regarded their own light drizzle as one more link with the homeland.

For there, at long last, was the royal liner at her berth at Central Wharf, and in a moment their Queen would be amongst them. Don Donaldson, New Zealand radio commentator, caught the tense emotion of the moment as he saw Her Majesty walking down the gangway towards the Governor-General, Sir Willoughby Norrie, who, with Mr. Holland and the members of his cabinet, stood waiting on the quayside. Carefully he counted the number of steps that remained for her to take. "Four, three, two, one"—then out came his exultant shout—"She's in New Zealand!"

It was the first time that a reigning British monarch had set foot on New Zealand soil, and all that reserve on which New Zealanders sometimes pride themselves melted before the grace and charm of Her Majesty's presence. There were cheers all the way from the official reception at the wharf side, up through densely packed Queen Street to the Town Hall, and a great wave of acclamation as the Queen took her place on the dais which had been built before the Town Hall at the top of Auckland's main thoroughfare.

Waving farewell to Queen Salote on leaving Tonga

Being greeted by Sir Willoughby Norrie just after arriving in New Zealand

Smiling happily the Queen prepares to address the vast crowds in Auckland just after her arrival

The cheering thousands stood in absolute quiet as they heard the clear, confident voice of their Queen thanking the city for it's memorable welcome. "Can you wonder that I am proud to be here?" she said.

Then delighted cheers broke out again as Mr. Holland placed a plastic mackintosh over the Queen's shoulders when the drizzle thickened for a moment. The Queen turned and smiled. "Thank you, Sir Walter Raleigh!"

This was the beginning of Auckland's five crowded royal days, and every one of them brought something new to the city's story.

On the very day of the royal arrival came the Garden Party at Government House, which managed to recreate the atmosphere of a similar function in far distant Buckingham Palace, in spite of the intermittent rain. There were other social events of importance including the royal visit to flower-decked Ellerslie Racecourse, where the Queen saw the race for the

Royal Auckland Cup, and the Auckland ladies gave a memorable display of courage by defying the rain and wearing their loveliest dresses in honour of Her Majesty.

But those five Auckland days gave everybody a chance to see and meet the Queen. The royal visitors walked through the wards of the hospital. They drove unannounced through the outer suburbs, and they received an ecstatic welcome from thousands of excited children in the green amphitheatre of Auckland's Domain. Even the weather relented at last, and the Queen and the Duke had sparkling sunshine as they crossed in their launch to the naval base of Devonport to present new colours to the young Royal New Zealand Navy. They saw the 'Queen City' from the water front, and Aucklanders were happy that their city had finally shown its best face to the Queen.

On her side, I think that the Queen will remember Auckland as the city where, for the first time in her life, she spent her Christmas away from Britain and from the happy gatherings of the family circle. Christmas Eve had been saddened by the news of the worst railway disaster in New Zealand's history. The Queen had immediately sent her message of sympathy to the nation, and later on the Duke of Edinburgh himself flew to comfort the relatives of the victims. Mr. Holland, the Prime Minister, expressed the wishes of the whole country when he asked the Queen not to break the schedule of the tour.

So, when Christmas Day dawned, Her Majesty did not disappoint boys and girls of the children's choirs of Auckland who had looked forward for months for their big moment—a concert of carols on the lawn before Government House. They sang all the old favourites, from 'Good King Wenceslaus' to 'Hark the Herald Angels Sing'. The Queen came out on the lawn to congratulate them and, in her turn, received a delightful surprise. Father Christmas himself appeared in a coach drawn by four tiny ponies. He bowed to the Queen and then dived into his magic sack and produced a rich variety of gifts for all present, including a walkie-talkie doll for Princess Anne and a train for Prince Charles.

There must have been a wonderful time at the royal homecoming when the Queen and the Duke produced the gifts given their children from all over the world. Auckland Harbour Road officials are, no doubt, wondering if Prince Charles has had a chance to try out their own gift on the lake at Buckingham Palace. It was a superbly finished small yacht the *Tui*, an ideal craft for a keen youngster learning to sail. Prince Charles heard all about it on Christmas Day, for the royal parents kept constantly in touch with their children by radio telephone, and in addition received special messages from Prince Charles and Princess Anne recorded on tape flown out from England.

After the excitement of the carols and the Christmas gifts, the Queen and the Duke drove to service at the Cathedral Church of St. Mary. Christmas dinner followed, and in the evening Her Majesty prepared for her Christmas broadcast. Here again history was being made. This was the first time the Queen had spoken to her people of the Commonwealth on Christmas Day from a point outside Britain.

A New Zealand investiture. "Arise Sir William Goodfellow"

All Nelson turned out to see their Queen

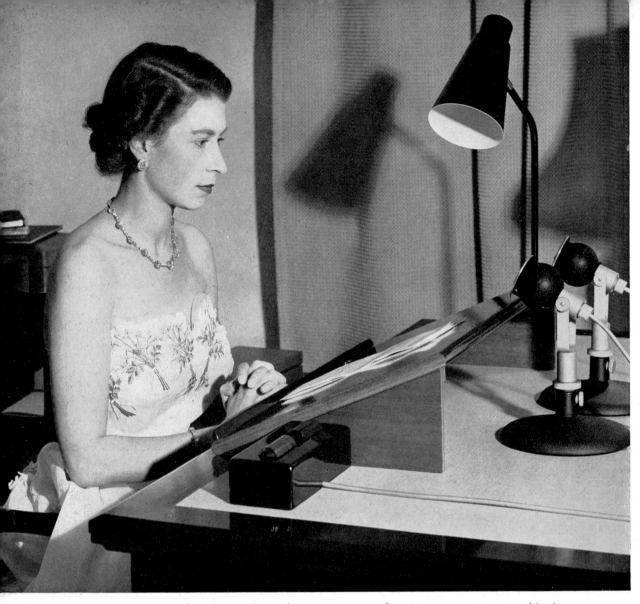

Her Majesty speaks to her people on Christmas Day 1953 from Government House, Auckland

As is her custom, Her Majesty had carefully studied her message, and sat alone before the microphone when the moment came for her to broadcast. The Queen is now a most accomplished radio speaker and has taken infinite pains to master the technique of the broadcaster. Her message was one of hope and confidence in the Commonwealth.

The Queen said, of our family of nations:

"Like New Zealand, from whose North Island I am speaking, every one of its nations can be justly proud of what it has built for itself on its own soil. But their greatest achievement, I suggest, is the Commonwealth itself, and that owes much to all of them.

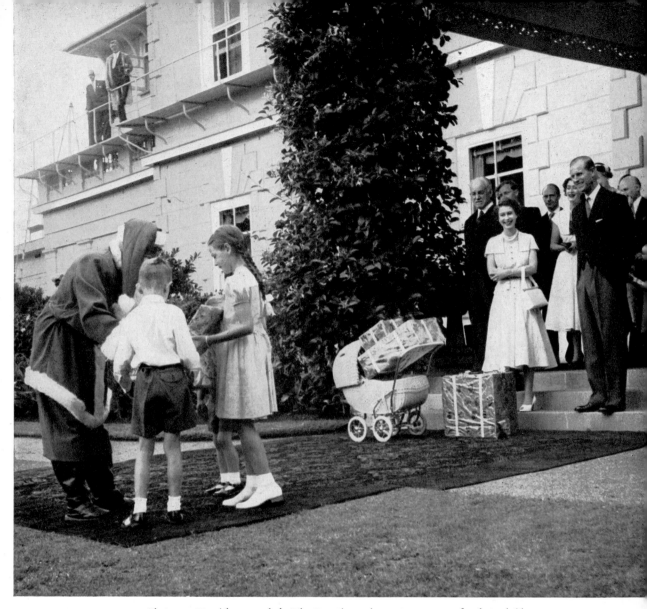

Christmas Eve 'down under'. The Royal couple receive presents for their children

Thus formed, the Commonwealth bears no resemblance to the empires of the past. It is an entirely new conception built on the highest qualities of the spirit of man: friendship, loyalty, and the desire for freedom and peace.

To that new conception of an equal partnership of nations and races I shall give myself heart and soul every day of my life."

On 28th December the Queen and the Duke left hospitable Auckland on the first stage of their journey through New Zealand. By Her Majesty's own wish the route was designed to include all the major centres of population. When the tour was being

"Yes-Yes. Here they come!"

discussed in London in the early stages of planning, the Queen's first question about any place was, "How many people are there?" She had no desire for her journey to be a tour of beauty spots, anxious though she might be to see some of the more famous of them. She had come to New Zealand to get in touch with the ordinary man and woman and throughout the strenuous weeks of her visit she was always aware of this deep, underlying purpose.

Those weeks were perhaps even more strenuous than had been anticipated. The Queen took with her a most loyal and

efficient staff, who certainly had no easy task. Both her ladies-in-waiting, Lady Alice Egerton and Lady Pamela Mountbatten had to be constantly on duty, ready to soothe over the difficulties that always arise on a royal tour. Much of the success of the visit was due to their unobtrusive work—and that of the rest of the royal staff—behind the scenes.

But however loyally they are supported, the main stress and strain of the tour must inevitably fall on the central figures, and especially upon the Queen. Her Majesty moves always under the intense and eager scrutiny of every woman who comes to meet or cheer her. New Zealand and Australian women pride themselves upon being among the best dressed in the world, and it was natural that they should want to see what the Queen was wearing.

They noted with lively interest a change in Her Majesty's taste during the tour. She tended to abandon pastel shades and prefer deeper and more sophisticated colours for her hats and frocks, although her hats in New Zealand still remained small and off the face.

Above all they were enchanted by the superb evening dresses Her Majesty wears so well and by the brilliance of her jewellery. She brought with her on the tour the most valuable collection of jewels ever taken out of England. Many of the pieces that caught the public eye, such as the diamond tiara she wore at the special session of Parliament at Wellington, were a personal gift to the Queen from her beloved grandmother Queen Mary. When she wore them on the great state occasions, Her Majesty was indeed the glittering 'faerie queen' of every New Zealand woman's dreams.

A happy Royal photographer

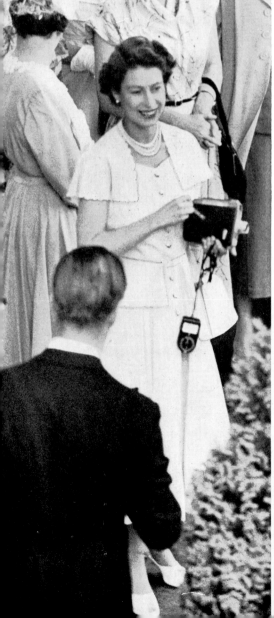

Watching the Ellerslie Races

But this is not how the majority of her New Zealand subjects will remember her. They will always see her as the smiling Queen with the gift of youth, simply yet perfectly dressed, who was never too tired to take a deep and genuine interest in every new place she visited and to touch it with the magic of her own vivid personality.

Northland was the first of the New Zealand provinces to greet the royal visitors. This narrow peninsula runs for three hundred miles north of Auckland. It is a land of rich farms and holds the few remaining kauri forests in the country. Its coastline is a maze of bays and waterways and on the shores of the most famous of these bays, the Bay of Islands, lies the historic shrine of Waitangi.

It was right that the Queen should visit Waitangi on the first possible moment after her landing, for this is New Zealand's Runnimede, the spot where the treaty was signed in 1840 by which the Maori chiefs accepted the authority of Queen Victoria. As the Queen stood before the white-walled Treaty House, which was restored by Lord Bledisloe when he was Governor-General from 1930 to 1935, she was greeted by the Maoris of Northland with all the traditional ceremonies of welcome. Maori and 'pakeha' are now members of the same nation with equal rights and owing a common loyalty to the Throne.

From Waitangi the royal route led back through Wangarei and Auckland and south into the Waikato Valley. At every point of the way the Queen saw a pattern of the welcome that was to be repeated all through rural New Zealand. It was a greeting that came from the heart and seemed all the more spontaneous when the decorations were home-made. Little family groups stood at the roadside. The country farmers had covered their old cars with ribbons and filled them full of kiddies waving Union Jacks, some of the flags twice as big as the proud toddlers who carried them. Villages had clubbed together to build their own arches across the road. Some of these were of straw decorated with country produce, and one, at the Scottish settlement of Waipu, bore the Gaelic greeting, 'Ceud Mile Failte'. The children's pet clubs turned out in force and held up their pet lambs, decorated with ribbon, for the Queen's approval.

The township of Papakure was determined that Her Majesty should not miss its claim to fame. No less than three large paintings of snow-capped mountains on the roadside proudly announced that here was the home town of Sir Edmund Hillary, the conqueror of Everest.

There were, naturally, fine official decorations in all the bigger towns she passed, but it was these informal demonstrations that told the Queen what rural New Zealand was feeling about the royal visit.

The tour now entered the rich Waikato district, one of the most progressive dairy farming areas in the whole Dominion. Here the emphasis was rightly placed upon country pursuits and agriculture. At Alton Lodge Stud farm at Te Kauwata, where the Queen stopped for lunch, Sir James Fletcher, the owner, was proud to show Her Majesty the 1937 Derby winner Midday Sun, to prove that New Zealand breeders are maintaining the tradition of

TOP LEFT: *A visit to an amazing cave at Waitomo, on New Year's Eve*
RIGHT: *Small Maori boys entertain the Queen with a daring display of diving from the Whaka Bridge*
BOTTOM LEFT: *Accompanied by the Mayor, Her Majesty steps down from a finely crowned canopy at Band Rotunda*

Royal beauty and dignity charmed all at Wellington, Auckland, and Christchurch

the best British blood-stock. At Hamilton, the thriving capital of the Waikato, the Queen saw something characteristic of the New Zealand countryside—a demonstration of high-speed sheep shearing by the Bowen Brothers, who have both held world championships. They appeared before her in their regulation dress of woollen shirt, tweed trousers and sack moccasins, while they also wore the hall-mark of a shearer—the 'Bowyang', a leather thong tied around the leg to keep the trousers slack. They

Maori maids and a warrior perform a dance of honour at Waitangi

fascinated the Queen by shearing two full wool Romneys in perfect style.

The Queen and the Duke saw the New Year in at the Waitomo Hotel near the famous Waitomo Caves. This was one of the few purely tourist attractions that the Queen permitted herself to visit, but it is also a 'must' for every visitor to the Dominion. It can claim to be one of the most remarkable places in the world. The Queen's imagination had been fired by the descriptions of many of her friends who had already visited it.

Deep down in the heart of the caves is a water-filled grotto, and overhead in the darkness shine myriads of tiny lights which are reflected in the still water like the stars of the Milky Way. The lights come from

glow-worms, tiny insects with a fantastic life cycle that can only be completed perfectly under the strange conditions supplied by the grotto of Waitomo. Nowhere else in nature can such an eerie light be seen in the very depths of the earth.

The Queen spent an entranced hour with the Duke and Guide George Sear, floating in a small boat through the silence of the cave, and the Duke smiled when the guide explained that the female shone more brightly than the male.

The glow-worms were in magnificent form, as were the other natural marvel of the North Island that the Queen visited, the Thermal Region. The great geyser Pohutu threw up a tall plume of spray and boiling water as if in welcome of the Queen's

43

arrival at Rotorua. This is one of the great centres of Maori tradition and culture, and the tribes had assembled in force to honour their royal guests. They showed the Queen the 'haka haka' the traditional dance of welcome or defiance, and they danced it with all the furious energy of the past. Then the Maori girls sang a 'poi' song, in which they kept a light, coloured ball moving from hand to hand with effortless grace and skill. At Waitangi, in the early stage of the tour, some of the onlookers had felt that the Maori had not retained enough of his ancient customs. They forgot that the Maori is now a citizen of modern New Zealand and cannot live in the past. He has already given proof of his ability to take his place side by side with his European-born fellow citizen, the 'Pakeha' as the Maori calls him. At Rotorua the modern Maori shows his Queen that he could retain the best in his past culture and use it to meet the needs of the present day.

Guide Rangi, who must be one of the best known of modern Maoris, took the Queen on a tour of the strange, subterranean world that bubbles so close to the surface at Whaka Thermal Reserve at Rotorua. The Queen saw hot springs, pools of boiling mud, columns of steam rising in unexpected fountains from the warm earth. Then, in holiday mood, the royal pair drove to Moose Lodge on the shores of Lake Rotoiti.

Here five days were scheduled in the official programme as 'rest days', when the Queen was to do exactly as she liked in a house where everything was prepared for her comfort. The New Zealand people were the perfect hosts. No one disturbed the royal seclusion. Everyone in the Rotorua area was determined that the Queen should have a relax 'away from it all' and especially with the Duke at her side.

Those first busy weeks of the tour had shown New Zealand the importance of the role played by the Duke of Edinburgh. They had seen him as the Queen's 'right-hand' man who watched her every movement in public with careful attention, always ready to help to take the burden off her in the more trying moments of the day. They had begun to appreciate him for his own sake, for his easy, friendly democratic way, and for his quick appreciation of the lighter side of the tour. They liked the way he had noticed the little Maori children on the bridge at Whaka, and had set them off shouting with laughter, as they dived for his pennies to amuse the Queen. They enjoyed his capacity for gay, unexpected 'asides', and relished the way he replied to the Bowen Brothers' invitation to try his hand at shearing a sheep. "No thank you. I might nick it and we've had enough mutton on this tour!" They also realized that in addition to being the thoughtful husband and the perfect partner, he has a keen mind which would stand no humbug. Throughout the tour he was determined to find things out for himself, and he showed at the Waikato Power Station, and at the other projects and industrial plants he visited, that he was well informed on all points of modern scientific research. At the end of those first few weeks New Zealanders voted him not only Britain's best ambassador but 'a good bloke' as well!

RIGHT *The Queen is chatting to some of the delighted patients of Christchurch Hospital, and* BELOW *being presented to the Maori chiefs at Arawa Park, Rotorua*

There can be no long rest on a royal tour and January 6th saw the Queen and the Duke flying out over the forest-clad centre of the North Island to the East Coast. Again they found themselves in an area where agricultural development is fast and promising. They travelled by air and then by road through Gisborne to Napier and Hastings.

The winds were rough and boisterous, but by now the royal pair had established an intimate and friendly relationship with the public of New Zealand and the Queen was not a bit embarrassed when she struggled to make her speech at Gisborne and the wind nearly blew the papers out of her hand. She was far more concerned about the youngsters who were getting the dust blown into their eyes. The Duke in turn willingly obliged the crowd at Hastings when some of the public who were placed behind the dais couldn't see him. A lone voice shouted, "Hey Duke. Where's the Duke?" The Duke immediately walked through the official group and appeared smiling and waving at the back of the dais.

Napier gave the royal pair a rousing welcome. It was impossible to believe that

From Kaiti Hill the Queen points towards Gisborne where Captain Cook first set foot on New Zealand

the gaily bedecked city, alive with the excitement of the royal visit, was devastated by an earthquake in 1931. Today it can proudly call itself the 'Riviera of New Zealand'.

At Napier the visitors transferred to the royal train for the 260 mile ride to New Plymouth through Palmerston North. The journey took two days and for most of this time the Queen and the Duke were on the observation platform of the train. Lonely farmers' wives saw a slim figure in a summer frock of wedgewood blue and waved excitedly. Motorists raced alongside the train and riders on horseback tried to keep up with it and wave Union Jacks at the same time. Quarry workers near Hawkes Bay carved God Save the Queen in black lettering against white limestone. Again and again the train stopped at small country towns, and for five blissful minutes the children would get their chance to see the Queen. This was one of the most delightful of royal progresses, a flash-back to the days when all royal tours were done by train and maybe people had more leisure and chance to see Her Majesty.

It was fitting that on this train journey the Queen should spend the night at Palmerston North where the railway runs right through the main street. Again and again the crowds clamoured for the Queen to come out on to the balcony of her hotel.

Next day the route of the tour took the Queen through Wanganui towards the Taranaki plain, and for most of the way she could see the magnificent, snow-clad cone of Mount Egmont towering over 8,000 feet into the bright sunshine. Enormous banks of hydrangeas filled the platforms of every little town and 'whistle-stop', and it was through a countryside that seemed one mass of flowers that the Queen came to New Plymouth.

Perhaps it was the children at New Plymouth who stole the show, and we can let the scene at Pukekura Park stand as typical of the overwhelming welcome given to Her Majesty by the youth of New Zealand.

Eighteen thousand people had crowded into the natural amphitheatre which is the pride of New Plymouth, and they roared a wild welcome as the royal car drove in. The Queen and the Duke transferred to a Landrover, which went weaving in and out of the excited ranks of 5,000 children who filled the centre of the ground. They seemed to be moving in the midst of a sea of red, white and blue streamers. Every child had a close-up view of the Queen. "I was so near that I could have touched her," one little boy said afterwards, and then added proudly, "Only I didn't, of course." One New Plymouth resident who missed his chance to see the Queen consoled himself "It's the children's day, after all. They are the citizens of the future. They must see her first, so that they can remember it all." New Plymouth made certain that they did.

Meantime, away to the south, the capital of New Zealand prepared to receive the Queen. Wellington is built on a circle of hills that surround one of the finest deep-water harbours in the world. The city is a place of splendid views, of nobly placed government buildings and suburbs where the houses cling to the hillsides. It has long been the key city of the Dominion administratively and politically, and today

Driving down lines of hundreds of cheering school children at Pukekura Park, New Plymouth

The brothers Ivan and Godfrey Bowen will always remember the handshake they received after their demonstrations of sheep shearing at McLean Park, Napier

industries are growing rapidly in the Lower Hutt valley across the harbour to add to the city's importance.

In Wellington, as befitted the city's status as the capital, the most important of Her Majesty's engagements was the special session of Parliament.

The Queen and the Duke arrived by air from New Plymouth and took up residence in Government House as guests of the Governor-General. Government House is a comparatively modern building for it was finally completed in 1910, but it has already been the temporary home of many royal visitors including Her Majesty's own father and mother when, as Duke and Duchess of York, they visited New Zealand in 1927.

The weather was anything but royal on the first few days in Wellington and drenching rain fell on Sunday morning as the Queen drove to the Church of St. Paul's. Her Majesty has set an example of church-going throughout the tour, and has never failed to attend divine service wherever possible. Here in Wellington the congregation met in the old wooden church where the atmosphere was that of a small village church at home, as the Governor-General and the Duke read the first and second lessons. The splendours of state were forgotten in the common emotion of worship shared on a moving occasion in New Zealand's history.

Those splendours were more fully displayed on Monday when there were civic receptions and parades of ex-service men, which included a small but proud contingent of South African war veterans. Then came the State Luncheon at Parliament House where the Queen made a memorable

Chatting to disabled ex-service men, Christchurch   *Entering Parliament House, Wellington*

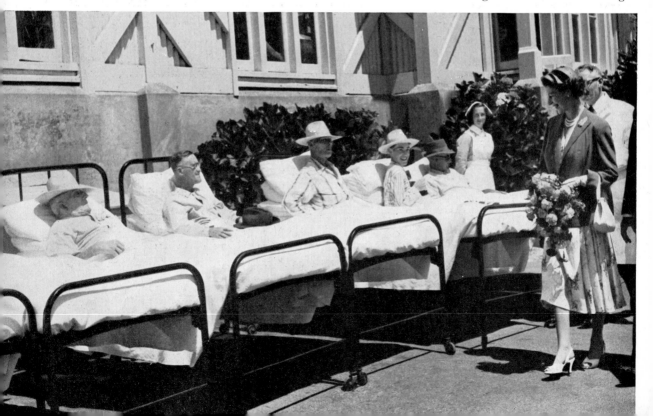

speech in reply to the Loyal Toast.

"This is a rich and lovely land," she said of New Zealand. "The progress that has been achieved in the comparatively short span of New Zealand's history bears witness to the vigour, courage and self-reliance of her people."

In a clear, ringing voice she again affirmed her faith in the Commonwealth.

"It is one of the great forces of good in the world, and the arduous times in which we live are a challenge to us to exert that beneficent influence with telling effect."

Her Majesty's opening of the special session of Parliament on Tuesday seemed to symbolize the unity of the Commonwealth.

ABOVE AND LEFT:
The scene inside Parliament House, Wellington during the State Opening of Parliament by Her Majesty the Queen who is seen wearing her jewelled coronation gown

RIGHT:
The Queen and the Duke of Edinburgh leaving Parliament House after the opening ceremony

Her Majesty with Privy Councellors after the meeting held at Government House, Wellington

Here was the Queen of England, who as also Queen of New Zealand, performing the same duty at Wellington as she had performed not so many months ago in the Mother of Parliaments 12,000 miles away across the other side of the world. Here were the same ceremonies generating the same emotions. And how regal Her Majesty looked as she entered the Council Chamber. She wore the fabulous dress that was made for her Coronation, rich in pearl, diamond and crystal embroideries. The Duke, in naval uniform, was at her side as she took her place on the gold and crimson throne on the dais. At such a moment—to those who watched and who had made the long journey with the Queen, those 12,000 miles seemed to vanish. Britain and New Zealand seemed to be one, close bound in a common loyalty.

Wellington's official ceremonies were worthy of the place and the occasion, but the royal visit to the capital city was not just a succession of noble and solemn occasions. The Queen and the Duke had a chance to see the industrial as well as the political and administrative side of the Wellington area. They went out to Masterton and to Lower Hutt and Petone. They visited a big motor factory and the Duke enjoyed the reply of a machinist who was sewing car fabric. "Do you do this kind of work at home?" smiled the Duke. "No sir," came the reply. "I leave it well alone."

The North Island of New Zealand had now paid its homage to the Queen and all the while the South Island, the 'mainland', as its inhabitants proudly call it, was waiting impatiently for its turn to show its

The Royal couple with the Prime Minister of New Zealand at the Regent Theatre

loyalty. The two islands are friendly rivals and are also sharply contrasted in scenery. The North Island is volcanic and well broken by hills and tracts of bush. The South Island is a country of snow-capped mountains and wide, rolling plains.

The Cook Strait that separates the two islands has a reputation for turbulence, and the Queen was well advised to fly across and make her first contact with the South Island at the thriving town of Blenheim. The royal Dakota touched down at Woodbourne Aerodrome, four miles outside Blenheim, at 12.15 p.m. and the Queen and the Duke drove to the central square. The scene was a familiar one by this time on the royal tour. The mayor waited on the special dais which had been built in the centre of the square surrounded by his fellow citizens. There were the usual cheers, presentations and address of welcome. But however often you have watched similar scenes, you cannot fail to be moved by the depth of feeling behind them. To the 8,000 people in Blenheim this was their day, even if it only lasted fifteen minutes. They had fought and pleaded for these precious minutes for in the original plan Blenheim was not a scheduled stop. The town had raced ahead with its decorations. They had placed an enormous crown on the bandstand in the square and hung garlands of artificial flowers along their streets. They will discuss for a long time to come every detail of the visit—from the bouquet of canna lilies presented to the Queen by the Mayoress, to the Duke's chat with Mr. Masefield, New Zealand's only Bisley

The enthusiastic welcome at Patea station where the Royal train made a stop

winner. As the Queen turned to wave good-bye, Blenheim was satisfied. It had lived to the full its one 'crowded hour of glorious life'.

The royal aircraft flew next to Nelson, where the Queen and the Duke stayed the night. They attended the Sunday service at Nelson's Cathedral, which stands on a dominating hill and which has probably the best position of any church in New Zealand.

Here the Duke broke away from the official programme to pay a surprise visit to the Cawthron Institute, New Zealand's most famous institute for plant and soil research. This visit is typical of the Duke's keen interest in the advancement of science. The Acting Director of the Institute, Dr. Miller had met the Duke earlier at a gathering of New Zealand scientists in Wellington. But one meeting was not enough for the inquiring Duke. He slipped away from the official programme and spent two hours discussing pest control and research into deficiency ailments in stock. Such visits give the Duke an unusually wide range of general knowledge. When he speaks to experts he can meet them on their own ground.

The note struck by Nelson was, on the whole, one of high purpose and serious endeavour. The next section of the tour was a complete contrast. The royal aircraft now flew down the rugged west coast to as wild a welcome as any that they had yet encountered. The West Coast prides itself on its open-handed hospitality. In the old days this was New Zealand's 'Wild West', and the spirit of the 'gold rush' and the 'diggers' still lingers amongst the native-born 'Coasters'.

The countryside is dramatic and impressive. Here the Southern Alps come close to the sea, and make Westland a place of deep forests, and rushing rivers, while away in the distance the great snow peak of Mount Cook, with all its attendant peaks and glaciers, rises over 12,000 feet into the southern sky. Her Majesty had a clear day for her flight and a superb view of the great mountain range on which Sir Edmund Hillary, the conqueror of Everest, received his early training.

Westport was first stop where the Queen was greeted by twenty minutes of concentrated ecstasy on the part of the children. Some of them had come from far within the mountain region and had never seen the sea or an aeroplane at close quarters before.

South to Hokitika, where the Mayor met them at the airport and they entered their car for the drive back to Greymouth. From Hokitika to the capital of Westland they had a real West Coast reception. They drove through the bush and along a wild and lovely sea-coast, to the climax at Greymouth where the crowd almost stormed the Queen's hotel in their enthusiasm. The smiling Queen came repeatedly on to the balcony, and the crowd stayed singing far into the night as they serenaded their Sovereign with the 'Sunshine of your Smile' and 'There'll always be an England'.

From Greymouth the royal route went by train through one of the great tunnels of the world, the Otira Tunnel, which cuts five and a half miles through the Southern Alps. The train paused to change locomotives at Arthurs Pass as it emerged from the tunnel, and that pause gave one New Zealand youngster the thrill of his life. He

ROYAL TOUR 1953-4

Chart of the Official Route

LONDON

MALTA

GIBRALTAR   TOBRUK

ADEN

ENTEBBE

COLOMBO

COCOS I^s

PERTH

ADELAIDE
MELBOURNE
HOBART

LEFT LONDON
Monday, 23rd November, 1953

ARRIVED BACK
Saturday, 15th May, 1954

Via GANDER

LONDON

TROPIC OF CANCER

BERMUDA

JAMAICA

EQUATOR

PANAMA CANAL

TONGA

E

TROPIC OF CAPRICORN

AUKLAND

WELLINGTON

LUFF

had carefully written to the Duke inviting him to come and play with his toy railway. The Duke had written back pointing out that it was a little difficult to upset the tour arrangements much as he would have liked to come and see the toy railway. Undeterred the youngster appeared on the station platform waving his toy engine, and the quick eye of the Duke spotted him. The result was a word with the Duke which made him the envy of all the youngsters of Canterbury province.

Christchurch was the next important stop. The capital of Canterbury province is proud to be regarded as the most English of all New Zealand's cities. It can also claim to be one of the most beautiful. It was laid out by the pioneer settlers in the 1850s along the winding banks of the smooth-flowing Avon, and its Gothic style public buildings are placed among green lawns and wide parks. In the heart of the city stands the cathedral, as English as if it stood in Canterbury itself.

Christchurch was worried by only one thing as it awaited the Queen. Would the citizens be even more English than the English and fail to let their loyalty break through their traditional reserve? They need not have worried. From the moment the royal couple set foot on the platform of Christchurch station all reserve was thrown to the winds. Never in the whole of the New Zealand tour have the crowds been bigger or more enthusiastic.

The royal visitors had hardly been ten minutes in their hotel before they came out on to the balcony. The city could not have given them a warmer welcome.

That warmth crept into every event of the royal stay. The Civic Reception took place in the Cathedral Square, where the mayor himself presented Her Majesty with the city's gift of a greenstone pen rack and then led his fellow citizens in three of the heartiest cheers yet given to the royal visitors. The Queen next called at the Christchurch Hospital, and again there was none of the formality and constraint that can sometimes descend on a royal visit. The Queen smiled, and the Duke stopped and talked in the children's ward to such effect that, when he looked up, he found that Her Majesty had disappeared. "Getting behind again," he chuckled and hurried to catch up on his schedule.

At five o'clock the Queen and the Duke attended evensong at the Cathedral where the singing of the choir lent a special beauty to the service, and the Duke's voice was relayed into the square as he read the second lesson.

There were three outstanding events on Wednesday. The Queen once again broke with long standing tradition when she conducted an Investiture ceremony in public at the Civic Theatre. In the past in Britain an investiture, especially that of conferring a knighthood, has usually taken place in the privacy of Buckingham Palace. But on several occasions in this tour this rule has been broken. The Queen has publicly conferred knighthoods and has allowed the ceremony to be photographed.

Thus in a young country a new precedent is created. Maybe that was what the Duke had in mind when he later addressed the Canterbury business men at lunch and described his visit to the Dominion as a 'breath of fresh air'.

The same pleasant informality marked the third event of the day, the garden party in the Botanic Gardens. The 3,500 guests had the company of the Queen and the Duke for half an hour more than was first announced. The Duke spotted an old friend in W. A. Hadley, who captained the New Zealand cricket team in Britain in 1949.

"How are you able to settle down again after the excitement of the tour?" he asked. Mrs. Hadley smiled as she answered for him, "He has to. We have four children."

The last day of the royal visit to Christ-church showed the visitors a sport with which they were unfamiliar. Trotting has become important in New Zealand and here in the Canterbury province is the headquarters of the sport. The Queen saw trotting at its best in the Addington course. In the evening she relaxed at the Royal Film Show.

Now it was 'Good-bye' to Christchurch with a visit to the major military base in the South Island at Burnham.

The Mayor reads the address of welcome at a civic reception held in the town hall, Wellington

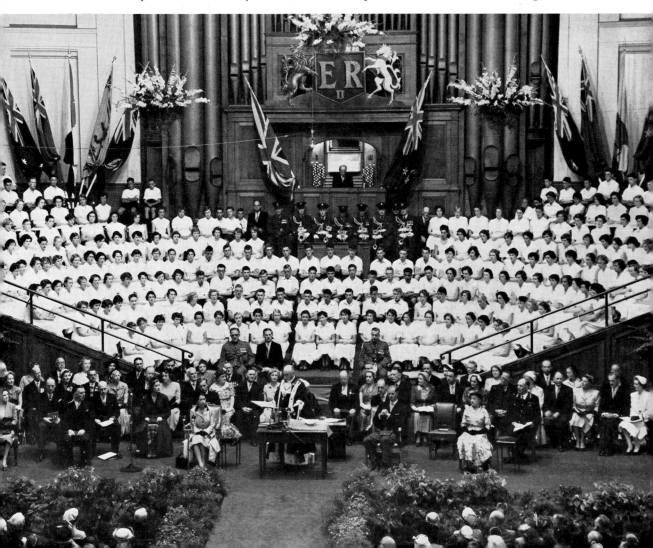

After the excitements of Christchurch came a short pause. The Queen rested at the famous sheep station of Longbeach near Ashburton. These periods of rest played an important part in the tour. They were so spaced that Her Majesty had a chance to recover quickly after each period of particular strain, and at Longbeach she found a home after her own heart. Since the early days of the settlement the station has been in the hands of the Grigg family. They have made the house into a typical English country house, where the windows look out on clusters of English trees, mirrored in the artificial lake and the still lily-ponds. There is even a private chapel attached, one of the very few in the Dominion. Around stretch the broad acres that carry over six thousand sheep. Her Majesty went riding and revelled in the peace of the place.

Then came the journey south and the final stage of her tour of New Zealand. These last few days in the South Island have a strangely moving quality about them. Maybe that quality came from the sense of the fleeting moments left on New Zealand soil and also from the character of the countryside through which the Queen was now passing. This is the part of the Dominion where the Scottish settlements were established. Dunedin is the 'Edinburgh of the South', and Invercargill youngsters still grow up speaking with a lilting Scottish accent. Here was their Queen amongst

LEFT: *Walking with the Mayor of Masterton and* RIGHT: *Talking with the Bishop of Christchurch*

The Duke leans across to assist his wife place a wreath on the War Memorial, Wellington

them, but to the folk of Southland she was their own 'Scotch Lassie' come home.

So the pipers played lustily for her at Dunedin and all the typical Highland Games events were staged before her at Invercargill. It seemed fitting that her reception at Balclutha should take place at the corner of Renfrew and Clyde Streets and that the woollen mill she visited at Dunedin should bear the name Roslyn.

And she in her turn was reminded of Scotland by the very appearance of Dunedin, set on the shores of what is surely a transplanted Highland loch and where the statue of Robert Burns stands in the famous Octagon square.

Invercargill hardly slept on the last night of the Queen's stay in New Zealand. She made her farewell broadcast from the hotel, and outside people sang with deep emotion, 'Will ye no come back again'.

Then, in the morning the royal travellers set out for the port of Bluff, the most southerly point reached by the Queen on the whole of the tour. Everybody who could crowded down to the harbour. People had slept out all night in their cars just to be on time to say farewell to the Queen. The *Gothic* was waiting at the quayside, and across the water from her a ferry boat full of the people of Stewart Island. Of all her subjects who greeted her on this tour, they must be the people who live furthest from her home in England. The entire population of the island had come across the rough waters of the Strait to salute their Queen.

The last 'Good-byes' were spoken. The Queen shook hands with Mr. Holland. This was 'journey's end' for the New Zealand tour, the end of six weeks of constant travel, 1,300 miles of it by car, 750 by aeroplane and 600 by train. But every one of those miles now had their memories for the Queen and the people of her proud Dominion of New Zealand.

The Queen went aboard. The *Gothic* moved slowly out of the harbour. Over the waters to the Queen and the Duke as they stood on the saluting dais on the *Gothic's* upper deck came the sound of singing. First the song of the Maori 'Now is the hour', then the song of Scotland that has also gone around the world, 'Will ye no come back again'.

There was not the slightest doubt in the minds of those who watched and waved on shore that soon Her Majesty would be back amongst them. "For now," as one watcher said, "We know that she really is Queen of New Zealand."

Pleasure radiates from the Royal smile as LEFT: *The Queen meets a cinema director, and* ABOVE: *Chats with a Samoan Boy Scout*

*The Queen and the Duke of Edinburgh making their last
farewells on the quayside of Bluff, New Zealand, before leaving for Australia.
Thousands of people cheered them as they left*

Chapter Three

AUSTRALIA

TO Sydney—bold, big, buoyant and one of the greatest cities of the whole Commonwealth—fell the honour of welcoming the Queen to Australia, and how nobly Sydney rose to the occasion! With nations, even more than with individuals, it's the first impression that counts, and the impression made by that joyous rip-roaring day when the Queen first set foot on the soil of Australia was overwhelming. Behind the cheering was the pride of achievement not only of a city and a state but a nation and a continent as well.

Sydney had the luck of the weather, of course. Never has the harbour looked better than on that warm, cloudless day of February 3rd, 1954, when the *Gothic* came steaming through the Heads. Thousands crowded to the shores and scores of small craft followed bobbing in the white wake of the royal liner. And it would be hard to match anywhere in the world the beauty of Farm Cove where Her Majesty landed at 10.30 a.m. on the gaily decorated pontoon

where the Governor-General, the Prime Minister of Australia, Mr. Menzies, and the Premier of New South Wales, Mr. Cahill, waited to receive her. The royal barge came slowly down through an avenue of gaily decorated yachts with the shining steel bow of the harbour bridge in the background.

The Queen stepped ashore not far from the very spot where Governor Phillip had landed at the very beginning of Australia's story over 160 years ago. Behind the green lawns and the trees of the Botanic Gardens that line the water's edge rose the tall buildings, the towers and spires of the great city, glittering with flags and banners. Past and present were here united as Her Majesty, after the official greetings were over, spoke for the first time on Australia soil, to her waiting people. "I want to tell you all how happy I am to be among you," she said, while all along the route ahead of her a million and a half Australian folk waited eagerly to prove to the Queen how

The Gothic *proudly steams towards* SYDNEY *while hundreds of little boats await the arrival of the Royal Party.*

The great moment has come at last—the Queen is on AUSTRALIAN *soil, and accompanied by Field Marshal Sir William Slim, Her Majesty advances to the Official reception followed by the Duke of Edinburgh.*

TOP: *Thousands of enthusiastic citizens line the route
to cheer their Monarch and her husband as they drive through Sydney*
BELOW: *With the Australian Prime Minister, Mr. Menzies, before Parliament House, Canberra, just
prior to the Opening of Parliament ceremony*

happy they were, also, to have her with them at last.

The royal drive through Sydney covered ten miles and every mile was a mile of triumphant cheering. London itself could not have outdone that welcome. Those of us who were fortunate enough to ride in the actual procession felt ourselves borne along in waves of joyous sound, while before us went the clattering mounted escort of the police. With them in the centre of this moving hurricane of cheers and waving flags was the royal car carrying the royal standard and the Queen and the Duke, smiling, waving and at moments almost overwhelmed by the warmth of their welcome. The procession drove under arches built with imagination. On one of them a gigantic log turned slowly to symbolize the timber industry. Another was formed out of four huge boomerangs. A third leapt from the four corners of a street intersection to support a glittering crown a hundred feet above the roadway.

But Sydney's finest decorations on that memorable morning could not have outshone the welcome given to the Queen in the little streets in the working-class quarters. Here mum, dad and the kids crowded the balconies so characteristic of the older Sydney houses and shouted "Give us a wave", and waved flags themselves until they almost broke the iron-work railings.

Sydney's first hour of the royal visit was probably its finest, but there was not a moment of the days when the Queen was in the city that wasn't filled with emotion and excitement. Sydneysiders crowded to see her wherever she went.

Her Majesty's programme took her to every part of the city and amongst every section of the community. She attended splendid official ceremonies such as the Opening of the New South Wales Parliament and the Investiture at Government House. This last occasion was a particularly happy one. For an hour the Queen bestowed honours on 127 men and 13 women

Some of the 120,000 children who met the Queen and Duke at the Sydney Cricket Ground

in the ballroom of Government House, crowded with the proud relatives of the recipients.

There were memorable speeches, too, including that of Mr. Cahill the Premier, at the State Banquet when he declared, "Our greatest pride is our loyalty to the British Crown." And never was that loyalty more vociferously displayed than at the Sydney Cricket Ground, the Show Ground and the Concord Oval when 120,000 children roared their greeting to such effect that the sound was heard miles away across the city traffic. One old hand on the Cricket Ground declared. "It beat the ovation we gave Bradman for his hundredth century hollow."

Looking back on that first hectic week of the royal arrival in Sydney it seems incredible that the Queen and the Duke succeeded in fitting in so many engagements in so short a time. They toured the North Shore and visited the Repatriation General Hospital. The Duke inspected the University while the Queen lunched with the representatives of the women's organizations. The royal visitors were together again at the State Ball and the concert at the Tivoli, where they saw opera and ballet by two of Australia's leading composers, Arthur Benjamin and John Antill. They visited Legacy House and had a glimpse of the unique way in which Australia has cared for her war widows and orphans. Legacy is no cold formal charity. It demands constant and personal service from specially selected leaders of the community. The Duke handed to the President of Sydney Legacy a cheque for £1,500, the proceeds of the special book compiled by Australian writers in Britain in honour of the Queen's visit to their native land.

In the midst of these pleasant and important duties, the Queen and the Duke also had a chance to see something of Australian sport at its best. The Queen, as a racing enthusiast, was delighted with her visit to the famous Randwick racecourse. Australians are keen racegoers, and every little town throughout the Commonwealth has its course in which it has a fierce local pride. Every racing man who could be there rushed to Randwick which became "Royal" Randwick for one glorious afternoon, when Her Majesty herself presented the trophy for the £10,000 Queen Elizabeth Stakes.

The Duke, it must be admitted, hasn't quite the same interest in racing as the Queen. He slipped away from Randwick and paid a surprise visit to the Sydney Cricket Ground, where he found himself in his element. He gaily dodged sitting in the isolation of the Royal Box, and took his place among the members in front of the pavilion. Western Australia were batting against New South Wales in a Sheffield Shield match. The crowd on the famous "hill", the traditional home of the wittiest cricket barrackers in the world, were delighted to see the Duke, and immediately shouted an invitation to "Come on and bowl".

After the cricket and the races the Royal Visitors drove to Bondi Beach where they revelled in a sport that is typically Australian, a surf carnival. The sun was warm and the surf ran high as the parade of life-savers stepped out over the yellow sands

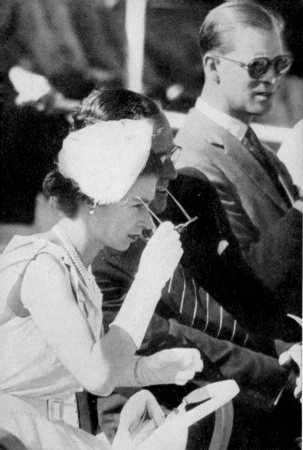

ABOVE: *A Sydney firework portrait thrills by night*
LEFT *and* BELOW: *The Queen adjusts her sunglasses to view the exciting surf carnival which took place at Bondi Beach*

During the ball held by the Lord Mayor of Sydney in honour of the Royal Visit

in a splendid array of bronzed bodies, brightly coloured costumes and waving banners. Thrills and spills came fast and furious when the surf boats rowed out to meet the 20-foot breakers, and the country's finest surfers came riding into shore on the top of giant Pacific rollers. The Queen was fascinated by the jargon of surfing which was explained to her by the Association President. A roller that flings you off the top is a "dumper", while the unfortunate surfer who gets smothered in the foam is said to have "gone down the mine". In fact, Her Majesty was so interested that she

stayed an extra forty minutes at the Carnival.

In those forty minutes the people of Bondi were able to take a longer look at their smiling, carefree Queen and to set their minds at rest on a question which had been worrying not only Sydney but the whole Commonwealth. "Was the tour proving too big a strain for Her Majesty?" Bondi convinced even the most anxious of her subjects that the Queen was delighted with her Australian welcome and with the new experiences it was bringing her.

The Queen is well aware that a tour on

this scale is not to be lightly undertaken. She knows that from time to time she will have to face official programmes that will tax her power of endurance to the utmost—days when she must be constantly moving, smiling, hand-shaking, all the time under the fierce glare of public interest.

She therefore takes good care of her health, eats and drinks sparingly, and relaxes completely once she is away from the crowds. As a result she stood up triumphantly under a schedule which would have taxed the strongest of public figures. She was not unduly distressed by the heat of Fiji and Jamaica, and, of course, the Duke of Edinburgh was always at her side ready to help her immediately she showed the slightest sign of fatigue.

It was therefore no tired figure but a radiant Queen, eager to see and be seen by

TOP: *Her Majesty is about to speak at the opening of the New South Wales Parliament*

BOTTOM: *Leaving their first church service in Australia at St. Andrew's Cathedral, Sydney*

TOP: *Wearing her Corona-tion Dress, Her Majesty creates history by being the first reigning Monarch to open the Federal Parliament at Canberra*

RIGHT: *After Parliament had been opened, units of the Australian Forces with their Colours flying, marched past the Royal saluting base in pouring rain*

her subjects, who set out from Sydney on her first visit to the Australian country districts.

Even in the short trip through New South Wales the distances she had to cover were so great that she had to use the aeroplane as her chief method of travel. Again she was following Australian practice, for the Australians must surely be the most air-minded people in the world. The farmer out in the back-blocks thinks nothing of flying 200 miles to do his shopping, and the business man will take an air liner to Brisbane or Melbourne as casually as his London counterpart catches the 8.30 train from Surrey up to the city.

Newcastle was the first to welcome her— a city which in thirty years has become one of Australia's greatest industrial centres. Here it was fitting that the highlight of the royal visit was the Queen's tour of the Broken Hill Proprietary plant. Never has a steel works been so brilliantly dressed for the occasion.

On to Lismore where she had a delirious welcome in the rain, and met the only people on record so far in Australia who burst into tears on being presented to the Queen. They will certainly be excused when you consider their ages. The two little boys and their two sisters were three and a half, and the famous Sara Quads had driven 200 miles for their glorious moment of bowing and curtsying to Her Majesty. The Queen's smile set the anxious parents immediately at ease—that smile which one of Australia's leading women writers so aptly described as being "as valuable an asset as the Crown Jewels".

Casino was next on the royal list, and barely a few weeks after the royal visit the town, together with nearby Lismore, was devastated by the worst floods in Australia's recent history. The muddy waters swirled past the town halls and into the hotels and the rooms where the happy ceremonies of greeting had been held. The memory of the Queen's presence and her instant message of sympathy helped the stricken settlements to fight back and face the future with new hope as the waters subsided.

The Queen now flew south to Dubbo, entering a country of great level plains where the land is rich in corn and where, to the west, lie some of the finest sheep pastures in the Commonwealth. The Dubbo Show gave her a chance of seeing the pride of the New South Wales farmers in their Merino sheep, for she walked through one of the most unusual guards of honour yet planned for her benefit. The owners held their prize stock with backs turned, as is the custom in sheep showing.

But every place the Queen visited during her tour around New South Wales had something new to offer or some individual note to strike. At Katoomba, for example, she heard her first Australian "coo-ee", when she visited Echo Point high up in the Blue Mountains and Mr. Clive Evatt, N.S.W. Housing Minister shouted for her across the lovely Jamieson Valley. At Bathurst ornamental gates at the entrance to the town were flung open by two young pages as the Queen's car approached. On her visit to Wollongong, the great new industrial centre south of Sydney, she drove fifty-two miles along the coast road and half a million people cheered her along her way. At Wagga-Wagga, in the centre of the rich agricultural district of the Murrumbidgee Valley, it was again the agricultural show which was the high-spot and the special exhibition of boomerang throwing. There may be some broken windows in Buckingham Palace later on unless Prince Charles has mastered the technique with his special presentation boomerang! The Duke asked Joe Timbery, the aboriginal expert, if it was dangerous. Joe grinned, "Lord, the only thing you could kill would be yourself."

New South Wales had been the first of the six states of the Commonwealth to acclaim the Queen. Now her journey took her to the city that symbolizes the whole of Australia, the federal capital, Canberra.

Canberra is not only a capital city. It is Australia's boldest gesture of confidence in her future. When Parliament decided after Federation to build a completely new administrative centre in the lovely but still lonely countryside of the Monaro tableland in the western foothills of the Australian Alps, the young Commonwealth undertook a task which few countries have ever tackled with success. Canberra was laid out on the boldest scale. It was to be as beautiful and dignified a city as the modern science of town-planning could make it.

The plans are far from complete today. Canberra is still a city of civil servants, of wide unfinished vistas, fine buildings standing in open countryside and roads that begin with confidence and end around the corner in almost untamed bush.

But it is this very incompleteness that gives the place it's charm. There is space everywhere, and even the humblest building has a wide, green lawn around it. Trees line every avenue, and there is room to breathe and talk. The country spirit seems to be still living in the heart of the city, and Canberra must be one of the few capitals

Three aboriginal dancers   *The Queen and Duke at Government House, with the High Commissioners*

in the world where you can drive a mob of cattle within sight of the windows of Parliament and have no awkward questions asked in the House!

It was also the incompleteness of Canberra that made the royal visit so perfectly managed an occasion, for there was ample space to allow every ceremony to be staged on an impressive scale. Here, in her capital, Australia showed the world that she had long left her eager, brash youth behind. She was now a nation fully conscious of her important place in the world and behaving with a dignity that commanded respect and admiration.

The Queen and the Duke flew to Canberra on February 13th, for a stay of four full days, and the city's normal population of 30,000 dutifully doubled itself for the occasion.

Each day brought its highlights. Monday was memorable for the State Opening of

AT CANBERRA

TOP: *H.M. the Queen escorted by the Australian P.M., Mr. Menzies, leaving the banquet at Parliament House, Canberra*

LEFT: *After the Royal couple had laid a wreath on the Commemoration Stone at the Australian National War Memorial, the Queen stood by the Duke as he saluted*

Parliament, and here Canberra shared the emotion of the moment with the whole of Australia. For the first time in history the Federal Parliament was opened by a reigning monarch.

The Queen looked magnificent in her jewel-encrusted Coronation robe crossed with the blue sash of the Order of the Garter. She took her place in the Senate Chamber with the Duke of Edinburgh, in the white summer uniform of Admiral of the Fleet, at her side. Before her was the crowded chamber, glittering with uniforms and legal robes in a way that sent the mind back across the seas ten thousand miles to the House of Lords at the opening of Britain's Parliament. The links that bind the two Parliaments were even more strikingly emphasized when the Australian Usher of the Black Rod, dressed exactly as his British counterpart, in black velvet coat, black knee breeches and silver buckled shoes, summoned the members of the House of Representatives to attend at the bar of the Upper House.

Her Majesty then spoke from the Throne, and her words had a deep significance for all who were assembled before her.

"It is a joy for me today," she said, "to address you not as a Queen from far away, but as your Queen and a part of your Parliament."

Yes, that moment in the Senate Chamber made Her Majesty, in very truth, Queen of Australia.

Outside, in pouring rain, the Armed Forces of the Commonwealth—the soldiers, sailors and airmen of the Queen—were assembling for the most impressive parade of the whole tour.

Happily there was warm sunshine for the next day's ceremonies. First, Her Majesty drove to the site of the new Australian war memorial to the American dead in the Pacific war. The monument is a bold, towering shaft cased with aluminium, and crowned by the figure of the American eagle. Two eagles afterwards encircled it as the Queen spoke of the bonds between all the English-speaking people. With telling effect she quoted from Abraham Lincoln's Gettysburg address.

"It is for us, the living, rather to be dedicated here to the unfinished work which they have thus far so nobly advanced."

Again it was in a mood of solemn dedication that Her Majesty drove to the Australian War Memorial which dominates Canberra from its nearby hill. She walked past the quiet pool that lies between the strongly built stone walls in the heart of the Memorial and laid a wreath on the commemoration stone.

The afternoon was the children's, and they gave the Queen their traditionally delirious welcome as she drove around the Manuka Oval in her Landrover. As a delicate compliment to Australia she wore a simply cut dress of wattle yellow and a hat made entirely of wattle sprigs and grey-green foliage. "It was like a golden crown," said one excited youngster after the parade was over.

The State Banquet in the evening was the brilliant climax of a day of finely conceived ceremony. The Queen sat next to Mr. Menzies in Parliament House, and, before them, 500 over picked guests. The Prime Minister had a delightful

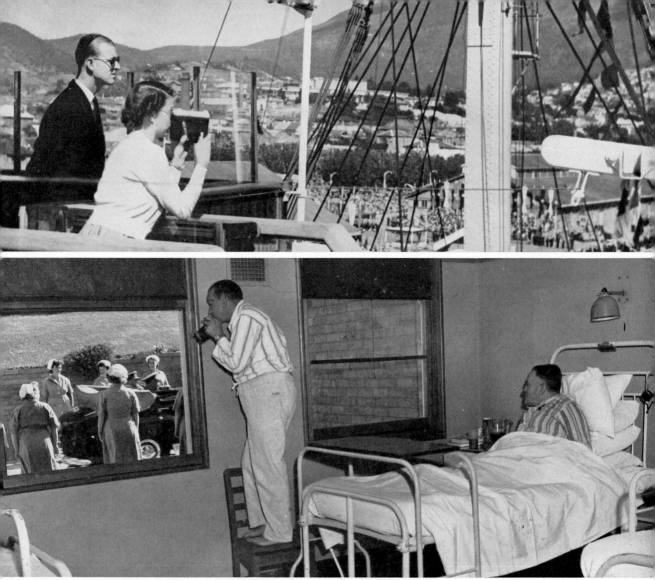

TOP: *The Duke of Edinburgh watches by the Queen's side while Her Majesty films the scene at Prince's Pier, Hobart, as the liner Gothic arrives at Tasmania*

CENTRE: *An ex-serviceman in the Repatriation General Hospital, Hobart, hops out of bed to snap the Queen and Duke of Edinburgh on their visit to the hospital*

BOTTOM: *Leaving the City Hall, Hobart, at the conclusion of the Civic Ball held in honour of the Royal Visit*

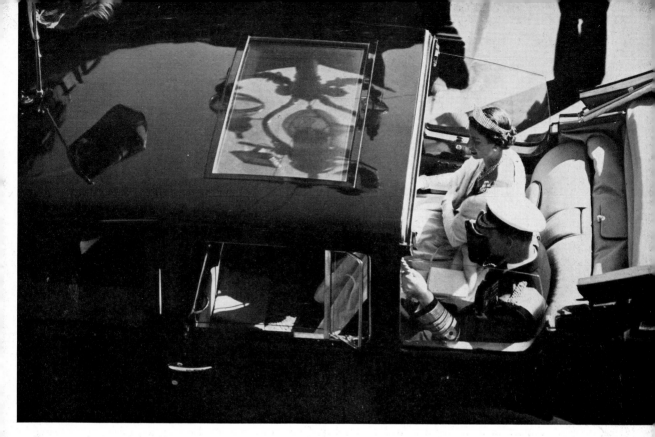

Melbourne welcomes its Royal Visitors

surprise in store for Her Majesty. She has a love and knowledge of fine jewellery which she inherited from her grandmother, Queen Mary, and it was with real pleasure that she received from Mr. Menzies, a diamond brooch spray, the gift of the Government, the Parliament and the people of Australia. The design—carried out in beautifully matched golden diamonds and blue-white brilliants—consists of a number of sprays of wattle, the Australian national flower, linked in the middle by three ti-tree flowers. It has already become a favourite with the Queen and she has worn it on many public occasions in Australia.

She in her turn made a gift to Australia of confidence and inspiration, when she spoke from the banquet, over the air, to the people of the Australian Commonwealth.

"This is a spacious country with a healthy and vigorous people and vast natural resources. Only a pessimist would set bounds to its future."

Australia thrilled at the Queen's praise, for these royal speeches on great occasions have been no formal collections of polite platitudes. Her Majesty and the Duke strove to use words that would inspire and remain in the memory. When the Queen referred to Australia as the 'promised land' for those with skill and enterprise in the old world, those who listened knew that she had felt deeply her responsibilities as ruler of a young and eager country.

Gay carnival-like scenes in the streets of Melbourne during the visit of the Queen

"You know," one woman said after the broadcast, "I've always talked about Australia as being a grand place, but I've never really felt it until the Queen spoke."

The effect of those royal words of encouragement will remain long after the pageantry and the excitement of the royal tour have ended.

On 18th February the Queen was back in twice-lucky Sydney to board the *Gothic*.

The royal liner moved slowly down harbour with its escort of little ships, past the hundreds of thousands of Sydney citizens, watching and cheering on shore. The last shouts of "Come back again" drifted across the blue water as the white ship passed the Heads and turned south in the evening light. The twelve wonderful days of New South Wales's welcome lay astern.

Tasmania is the smallest of the states of the Commonwealth, but it is fiercely proud of its eventful history and refers to the rest of Australia as the mainland. It is an island of farms and orchards, of great sheep runs and wild densely forested mountains in the interior. And it is small enough for everybody in Tasmania to have had a chance of seeing the Queen.

As a result the royal tour of Tasmania had an easy charm about it, and Her Majesty relaxed from the moment the *Gothic* steamed up the magnificent fiord that leads to the capital. Hobart is a city of old stone houses, where all streets seem to end at the Quay. Behind it Mount Wellington stands sentinel, a 4,000-foot peak clothed in woods and with a motor road curving to the top.

The Queen arrived at a happy moment in Hobart's history for it was the 150th Anniversary of the foundation of the city.

She had a further reminder of Tasmania's links with the past when she opened the State Parliament. The Legislative Chamber

is small but dignified and is dominated by the full-length portrait of Queen Victoria in her Coronation Robes. As the Queen, dressed in a white, thin, corded-silk gown, rose to make her speech she glanced at the portrait of her great-great-grandmother. At a moment like this the long eventful years between the two reigns seemed to fade, and the unbroken continuity of our history was revealed.

Government House, where the Queen stayed with Sir Ronald and Lady Cross, is again a home which guards this precious continuity with the age of Victoria, for its baronial battlements, its gothic windows and the surrounding lawns gay with formal flowerbeds give it a period charm.

The grounds slope down to the River Derwent, which is crossed by the graceful, curving pontoon bridge and backed by wooded hills. No Government House in the whole of Australia can rival these lawns as

a setting for a garden party and maybe the sheer beauty of the place made the Hobart party go with a swing. The Duke enjoyed himself so much in chatting to the guests that the Queen had to begin the presentations without him. There was general laughter as he came hurrying up to make his apologies and join Her Majesty.

There was no possible room for doubt that in all these ceremonies Hobart had made the Queen feel really at home.

She was reminded of home in a different way when, on 22nd February, she flew to Northern Tasmania. There is no countryside in Australia more English in appearance than the lovely coastline from Wynyard, along the Bass Strait, to Launceston. It is a pattern of rich fields backed by wooded hills. There were moments when the Queen exclaimed "Why, we might be in Kent!" The royal car drove through little towns and villages and past sandy bays where the children ran from the warm water to cheer their Queen in their bathing costumes. Litte girls in Dutch costume sang a song of welcome as the royal car passed, for this is an area where many new Australians have settled and, for the new settlers not only in Tasmania but all over Australia, the tour has been a great opportunity to show their loyalty to their new country.

Australia needs a constant stream of immigrants if she is to develop her magnificent heritage, and the Queen's journey has spotlighted the country and the opportunities it offers. There will be an undoubted increase in applications for permission to sail to this new 'promised land' of the south.

While the new Australians cheered, one of the oldest Australians stood on the

Fine illuminated decorations enliven 'Royal' Melbourne at night

roadside near Penguin and saluted. He was Mr. William Hunt, aged ninety-nine and Australia's oldest surviving soldier. The veteran stood proud and firm as he fulfilled his dearest wish. "I've served Queen Victoria," he said, "and now I'm determined to salute her great-great-grand-daughter. Long live the Queen!"

The Queen spent the night at Connorville, one of the historic houses of Tasmania.

Rested and charmed, the Queen and the Duke motored next morning to loyal Launceston. Their aircraft took off from the airport outside the city, and circled over the hills of Tasmania for the last time. Victoria, and its capital, Melbourne, were an hour and a half's swift flight away. "This city," said a Melbourne man on the morning of the Queen's arrival, "is suffering with pleasure from a bad attack of

The Argus, Melbourne

DUKE OF EDINBURGH VISITS MELBOURNE UNIVERSITY

ABOVE: *Seated on the memorial chairs with the University Chancellor Sir Charles Lowe*

TOP LEFT: *Being presented to the various professors, masters and officials of the University*

CENTRE LEFT: *Ragged by the students he receives a somewhat outsize 'key to all knowledge'*

BOTTOM LEFT: *The Duke amused by student John Thompson disguised as a University vamp*

BELOW: *A moth-eaten carpet is ceremoniously rolled out*

Her Majesty enjoys the beauty of the begonias in Ballarat's beautiful Botanical Gardens

Queen Fever. You can feel the temperature rising!" Indeed you could, for the city had 'gone gay' long before the royal aircraft touched down at Essendon airport.

Now between Melbourne and Sydney there is a long-standing but friendly rivalry. Sydney had done magnificently. Melbourne determined to do even better. Who could decide between the two? Certainly not Her Majesty the Queen, who found herself cheered to the echo from the very moment she landed.

When a great city like Melbourne becomes host to the Queen, it does things in a big way. Nowhere in Australia were the decorations more lavish, the crowds more excited or the fireworks and illuminations at night more splendid. From dignified Collins Street to busy Bourke Street and out along the open parklands that lie, as a tribute to the foresight of the city fathers, beside the winding banks of the Yarra—everywhere there were flags and triumphal arches. There was only one more flag needed to complete the decorations, the Royal Standard itself. When the citizens of Melbourne saw this richly emblazoned symbol floating at the mast head high over Government House, they felt that their happiness was complete.

The official programme for the royal visit was a crowded one. The Queen spent sixteen days in all in the State of Victoria and seven of these in the city of Melbourne. Each of these days seemed to have its individuality clearly marked. The 25th February, for example, was a day of formal splendour, when the Queen opened Parliament. The crowd saw her walk with that effortless grace and dignity which is her own special secret on State occasions, up the long flight of steps leading to the Parliament House—a slim figure, clad in shining silk set off by the deep blue of the ribbon of the Garter. This is just how the women of Melbourne had imagined the Queen would be.

She retained that grace when she attended the rally of ex-service men and women on the Melbourne Cricket Ground, and those who were there will never forget the emotion of the moment when the huge crowd sang 'God Save the Queen' and sent their voices, a hundred thousand strong, sounding over the listening city.

The 27th was a day set aside for sport, and the Queen drove to Flemington Racecourse, Melbourne's pride, and the best-known course in Australia. Here the Australian Derby, the Melbourne Cup, is run and the whole of the Commonwealth stops to listen. The whole of Australia also seemed to have done its best to squeeze into the ground, as the royal car made its slow drive up the straight, accompanied by its escort of mounted police and bringing an air of Royal Ascot to Flemington. Her Majesty does not, of course, place bets upon the runners, but she had the pleasure of picking the winner, Cromis, in her own Queen Elizabeth Stakes.

The Duke, meanwhile, had gone to the Kooyong Tennis Courts where the Queen joined him after the races in time to chat with the Davis Cup players.

Sunday was a day of significant ceremony. As is her custom, Her Majesty attended divine service at St. Paul's Cathedral in the heart of Melbourne, and then drove through the lovely parklands that border the Yarra to the Shrine of Remembrance. The huge crowd that had gathered before the steps leading to the central shrine and the new forecourt stood in reverent silence as Her Majesty made her speech of dedication, and then pressed the button to light the flame that will burn in perpetuity in its bronze bowl before the shrine as a memorial to the men and women who gave their lives in the Second World War.

No doubt 4th March was also planned as a day of ceremony, but youth took charge and swept formality away with some of the most spontaneous laughter yet heard on the royal tour. The Duke arrived at Melbourne University to be officially greeted by the Chancellor, Sir Charles Lowe, but no sooner had the royal visitor appeared than the architectural students rushed a giant imitation television camera, christened the 'murkmaster', on to the scene. A mock running commentary accompanied the Duke, a guard of honour presented T-squares, while students in fancy dress rolled out a moth-eaten red carpet before him. The Duke enjoyed himself up to the hilt and turned the tables a little later on when the Chancellor presented him with a handsome blotter as a memento of his visit. "This will remind me not to blot my copy book," smiled the Duke.

The days of the royal visit to Melbourne were crowded but the evenings rivalled them in glamour. The city didn't mind tangling itself up in gloriously good tempered traffic jams as the crowds rushed to cheer the Queen at the Lord Mayor's Ball or at the glittering command performance of the *Tales of Hoffmann* in the Princess Theatre. Thousands stood in the streets to hear the opera over loudspeakers and to catch a fleeting glimpse of the Queen as she left.

Her Majesty waves happily after watching a film première 'down under'

The Queen replies to the Lord Mayor's speech of welcome at Sydney shortly after setting foot on Australian soil

Above all, the women of Melbourne were fascinated by the dresses worn by Her Majesty. "How perfectly she chooses her dress to suit the occasion," was one comment, and a prominent woman commentator praised the Queen for making sure that her dress never clashed with her background. 'A tailored ensemble for tailored Melbourne,' in particular, earned universal approval.

But few realized the careful planning that lay behind the cool unruffled elegance that the Queen always seems to achieve on her public appearances. Her Majesty always has the final choice, but her dresser, Miss Macdonald, has to be ready with practical advice on the colour and style of the dress to be worn on any particular day. The Queen took over a hundred dresses with her on the tour, and Miss Macdonald studied the type of road on which the Queen was to travel and the colour of the formal dais and even the flowers with which it would be decorated before she made her recommendations. Hats commanded the same careful attention as dresses, and Her Majesty followed, in Australia, the style that she favoured in New Zealand. She knew that there were thousands of women eager to see her, and so her hats were always 'off the face'.

Melbourne had a right royal view of the Queen but the city did not monopolize the royal visitors. It was the centre from which Her Majesty and the Duke toured the rest of the state. The Duke made a special visit to the Flinders Naval Depot, where he took the parade on a ground that for sheer beauty must be unique amongst the naval establishments of the Common-wealth, and then had a chance for a chat and a drink with some of his old comrades of his service days in Australian waters.

Both the Queen and the Duke enjoyed a carefree rail journey through the country districts of the state. They went through the grazing country of Seymour and Benalla, on through Bendigo and Ballarat to Geelong. Ballarat, in especial, counted itself lucky, for the city held its reception in the Botanical Gardens. Now the hothouse contained a superb display of begonias, which were not included in the official programme. The people of Ballarat, however, longed to show them to the Queen, and the loudest cheers of the day occurred when Her Majesty turned back to see the flower display. Ballarat felt that it had been well and truly put on the map.

Victoria also took care to give its visitors a chance to rest, and the Queen and the Duke spent a few days away from the crowds in the chalet of O'Shannassy Lodge deep in the mountains of the Great Dividing Range. Here they saw the real Australian bush at close quarters, for the lonely forests were loud with the music of the bell birds and the chuckling note of the kookaburra. Ahead of the Queen now lay the long flight direct from Melbourne to Brisbane, the capital of Queensland.

Queensland was undeniably anxious about the royal visit. The second largest state in the Commonwealth is second to none in its loyalty to the throne. "Queensland is the Queen's own land," the premier, Mr. Gair, declared, but the state faced the problem that the royal visit coincided with the rainy season. Other states could rely on sunshine for the Queen's progress but

A MELBOURNE SCRAPBOOK

ABOVE: *With an escort of Victorian Mounted Police
Her Majesty arrives at Flemington Race-
course to see Australia's classic race, the Melbourne Cup
Is the Queen picking the winner?*

LEFT: *Enjoying a quiet week-end, their Royal Highnesses
pose on the steps of the veranda of O'Shannassy Chalet,
Warburton*

TOP RIGHT: *Tennis usherettes form a guard of honour
to greet the Queen's arrival at Kooyong Tennis Courts
which is the Wimbledon of Australia where Hoad,
Rosewall and Hartwig defeated America to retain the
Davis Cup for Australia in brilliant style in 1953*

BOTTOM RIGHT: *The master mind that has done more
than anyone to make these famous Australian victories
possible is trainer Harry Hopman a former champion
in his own right who is seen here being introduced
to Her Majesty by Sir Norman Brookes*

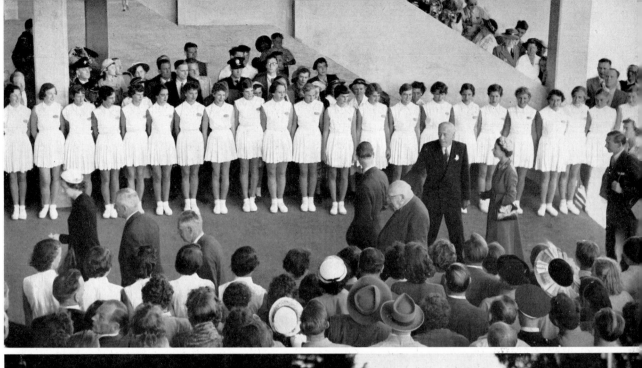

Queensland had already received more than its quota of rain before Her Majesty arrived. Some of the towns the Queen was to visit had been hit by hurricanes, others still had flood water in the streets of their suburbs, and few had had the luck of a week of clear sunshine in which to get their decorations in order. There had been landslips on the railways up north and thousands of people from the 'out-back' who had been planning for months to get down to the coast to see the Queen, were cut off.

But how magnificently they arose to the occasion! Their spirit was expressed by the Mayor of Cairns, when he declared, "As long as we get the Queen here we don't mind if we stand up to our necks in water to see her!"

Happily there was no need to do that, for the rain relented and the Queen landed in Brisbane in brilliant sunshine.

As soon as the royal car left the airport and started on its drive towards the centre of Brisbane, it was clear that Queensland's welcome was going to be 'different'. The very crowds had a tropical air about them —gay, free and easy, dressed for the sun. Great banks of red cannas made the gardens royal with colour. There was music all the way, from the pipe bands in full Scottish regalia to the little family bands that appeared in the suburbs and made the Queen and the Duke laugh with enjoyment.

Mum, Dad, and the kids had all brought out a drum or a trumpet and made a gloriously loyal din! But Brisbane's noblest moment came a little later as the procession entered the Exhibition Grounds for the civic welcome. Those of us who rode behind the royal car will never forget the thrill of hearing 'Land of Hope and Glory' sung by the massed choirs in white and accompanied by the state orchestra. The sound soared over the crowded oval and echoed through the loud speakers over the whole city.

Brisbane was a dream city that evening. The great bridge over the river was outlined in light, and cheering people ran alongside the car as the Queen drove to the state reception at the Parliament House. Again here was something in which Queensland was different. The state is the only unicameral legislature in the Commonwealth of Australia so Her Majesty was not received in an upper house. Instead, after the official speech of welcome and her reply, the Queen walked with the Premier amongst the 1,500 guests, while outside the stars sparkled in a perfect tropical night sky.

Queensland also held a record in the distance that the Queen covered by air in the state. The area of Queensland is so vast that air travel was the only practical solution of the problem.

In her comfortable Quantas Constellation, with its cabin decorated in restful pastel shades, Her Majesty flew to Bundaberg and then across to Toowoomba, places that are separated by over 200 miles of plains and heavily forested mountains. Tree-lined Toowoomba claims to be the most beautiful city in Queensland. It produced two surprises.

The little two-year-old son of one of the councillors wandered unconcernedly on to

The Queen with her Ministers at Government House, Melbourne. FROM LEFT TO RIGHT: *Mr. McEwan (Minister for Commerce), Mr. Holt (Minister for Labour), Mr. Menzies (Prime Minister), Dr. Evatt (Opposition Leader), Mr. E. J. Holloway (Former Labour Minister), Mr. R. G. Casey (External Affairs), Sir Michael Adeane (Private Secretary to the Queen) and Mr. A. S. Brown (Secretary, Prime Minister's department)*

the royal dais, to the evident delight of the Duke, and a group of Australian aborigines performed their corroboree dances before the Queen. They came from the centre of Australia and from the Northern Territory and their dance, with its imitation of the movement of the kangaroo performed to the deep bass note of the bamboo pipe called a 'didgeridoo', carried the spectators back to those remote, far-off days when the Great Southern Continent was still a mysterious legend. It seemed to make even more impressive Australia's achievement in building a modern nation, with great cities and wide farmlands, in the short space of about 160 years.

Cairns was the furthest point north reached by the Queen in Australia. From this lovely tropical town she sailed in the *Gothic* for another visit which made this Queensland tour unique. She went out to the Great Barrier Reef, that fantastic line of coral reefs and islands that stretches 1,200 miles along the Queensland coast. The main barrier lies far out to sea and the Pacific thunders on to it in a perpetual welter of white foam. But within its protecting arms lies hundreds of smaller

ABOVE: *H.R.H. presents the Queen's Colours to a young lieutenant for the Flinders Naval Depot*
CENTRE: *Leaving the fine Shrine of Remembrance in Melbourne*
BELOW: *The Archbishop of Melbourne presented by Sir Dallas Brooks*

islands and reefs, each with its vivid, multi-coloured coral growth and its green forests that come down to the very edge of the crystal-clear water.

The Queen went ashore on the tiny Seaforth Island in the Cumberland group about fifty miles north of Mackay. The secret had been well kept and the royal party had the island to themselves. They lazed the day away in slacks and shorts, bathing and looking down from a glass-bottomed boat on the amazing fish that move like flecks of glittering tinsel amongst the coral. It was one of the most restful days of the tour, and when the Queen returned to the *Gothic* the ship moved south in a sunset that rivalled the coral in the boldness of its colour.

South to Mackay, where a tropical deluge lifted before the royal visitors stepped ashore, and then on to Rockhampton, gay and decorated in defiance of the flood waters that had so recently poured through its streets, to return at last to Brisbane and a thrilling 'welcome home'. Her Majesty had travelled 1,000 miles by air and 500 by sea on her Queensland visit, probably the most strenuous part of her tour. Queensland, true to her determination to strike a new note, had one final surprise for the Queen. Before they left, a selection of all the most characteristic animals of Australia were introduced to the royal couple and, as usual the animal that stole the show and came in for most of the royal attention was that enchanting, living 'teddy bear', the koala.

The royal Constellation took off from Brisbane on 18th March. The lush green of Queensland faded below as the aircraft flew out over western New South Wales and the sheep country. The land became drier, more arid. This was the real 'out-back,' and in its south-west corner amid the bare, rocky country west of the Darling River, is one of Australia's greatest mining centres, Broken Hill. The Queen went to the model mine of the Zinc Corporation and then drove to the Flying Doctor Base for one of the most human and moving half-hours of her Australian visit. She sat in the studio at the base and listened to the voice of Mrs. Mitchell of Muloorina station, speaking from 300 miles away in the north-west, in the midst of that desolate and lonely land that lies near the dried-out bed of Lake Eyre. Mrs. Mitchell told her of the life of the women in the 'out-back', and of what the Flying Doctor Service, pioneered by the Rev. John Flynn, meant to them. "Without this mantle of safety we mothers would not dare to bring up our families so far from medical help," she said. Across 300 miles of hard, tough country the Queen and one of her loneliest subjects were united in sympathy.

On the Melbourne Cricket Ground thousands of school children cheer their Monarch

The population of Brisbane turn out in full force to greet the arrival of the Queen and Duke at the City Hall.
A magnificent royal ball was staged here later
Scenes from the march-past rally of 17,000 ex-service men and women.   Well done, Brisbane!

Her Majesty herself had now to make a 300-mile journey to Adelaide and South Australia.

A wit once claimed that Australia was an archipelago made up of six islands, by which he simply meant that each of the states jealously guards its local independence and rights, above all the right to welcome the Queen in its own way. This was all to the advantage of the tour, for every time it crossed a state border it renewed its vigour. Queensland had struck a new note, but it mattered not a jot to South Australia what Queensland or Victoria or New South Wales had done. Her Majesty was on South Australian soil, and to South Australians it was as if she had landed on the continent for the first time.

As a result all the now familiar round of state balls, garden parties and children's gatherings took on a fresh sparkle.

Adelaide can claim to be the perfect city for royal occasions. It was laid out with remarkable foresight by its founder, Col. William Light, and he ensured that it should be surrounded by a ring of magnificent parklands. As you drove towards Adelaide on the night of the Queen's arrival, through the long avenues of trees, the whole city seemed to be made of light and to float free from the mundane earth. No capital beat Adelaide for the charm of its decorations and illuminations, for the city fathers concentrated on those simple but most evocative of colours, red, white and blue.

No city either surpassed Adelaide's children's gathering for spontaneous gaiety and for the distance that some of the children had to travel. One party came from the

'Private Septimus' a mascot belonging to the Royal Australian Infantry is proud of his new fan

very heart of Australia down the long railway line from Alice Springs in the famous train known to the whole of the centre as the 'Ghan', after the Afghan camel drivers of the old days. 'The town like Alice' gave the children a tremendous send-off as the *Royal Ghan* steamed out carrying a proud banner in front, '1,000 miles to see the Queen'. But even this record was broken by four youngsters who travelled from Port Darwin in the Northern Territory. They had covered 2,000 miles by the time they stood in Wayville Oval to greet the Queen.

Using Adelaide as a centre the Queen

and the Duke flew to Whyalla, South Australia's newest industrial centre and to Port Lincoln, one of its oldest ports. Then for a happy day in the wine districts of Renmark and Mildura in the reclaimed lands of the Murray Valley.

One royal occasion in South Australia stands out for its importance, not only to the state but to the whole Commonwealth. On 22nd March the Duke of Edinburgh flew to inspect the rocket range and the settlement of Woomera. Woomera lies far to the north-west of Adelaide on the edge of the enormous expanse of semi-desert that makes

H.M.A.S. Australia, the Gothic's escort ship is inspected by Her Majesty off Townsville

At Perth George Rogers seventy-three year old ex-rowing champion of Australia enjoys a 'royal chat'

up Central Australia. It is here that Britain and Australia have combined to test their rockets and atomic weapons, and no better place could be conceived for the purpose. The country is wild and lonely, and perfect for security. No stranger has a chance of getting in and out of it undetected. The little settlement of Woomera is in itself a marvel of efficient planning. A township has been created in the middle of a wilderness, complete with schools, clubs, playing fields and swimming pool. Water is pumped across the desert from the far distant Murray River and thousands of trees have been planted to surround the whole community with shade. But the range itself, twenty miles out from Woomera, is the real centre of attraction.

The Duke drove to it along the road that goes dead straight between its guardian lines of telegraph poles to the low ridge on the skyline that holds so many of our defence secrets. In a nearby workshop the Duke saw all our latest weapons—while the strictest guard was kept for any unauthorized visitor.

Then he stood on the observation deck of the new instrument-control building to watch the firing of one of the latest rockets. There was drama in the relay of the technicians' voices counting off the minutes, and as the last technician gave the go-ahead with a casual "When you like, Phil," the rocket seemed to leap from its launching cradle with a deafening roar to blaze a flaming trail 12,000 feet into the clear blue sky at over 1,200 miles an hour. It was the sign of the future burning over a landscape that had hardly changed in thousands of years.

TOP: *A Koala Bear is socially introduced at the Brisbane Ball*
CENTRE: *Head-dresses from the Torres Straits impressed the Queen*
BOTTOM: *H.M. driving through the tropical charm of Mackay*

NOW ADELAIDE

ABOVE: *Her Majesty and the Duke of Edinburgh arrive at Parliament House for the State Banquet*

LEFT: *A fine view of the State drive through the city*

BELOW: *The Queen who visited the Oval, Adelaide, is seen here being presented to the two teams just before the match began*

ABOVE: *The scene in Bonython Hall where the Queen met representatives from over a hundred South Australian women's societies*

LEFT: *The arrival at Parliament House where Her Majesty opened the second session of the Parliament of South Australia*

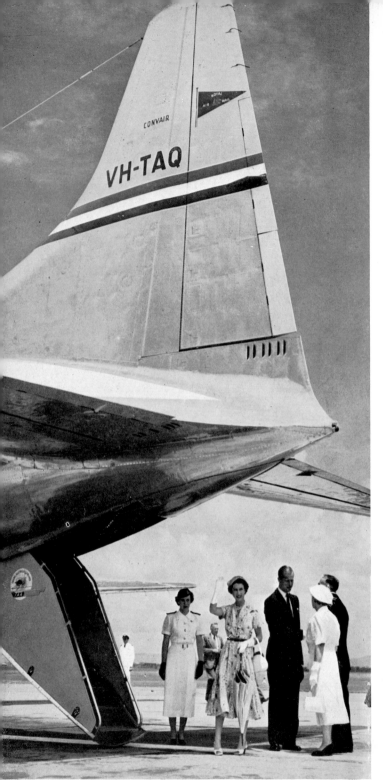

As the Queen waves good-bye the Duke shakes the Mayor warmly by the hand before leaving Mackay

Woomera is the spectacular open-air laboratory for our rockets, but behind it is the great base of Salisbury, outside Adelaide, where the planning and actual manufacturing is done. The Duke is nothing if not thorough and he balanced his exciting tour of Woomera by a sober, though provoking talk with the 'back-room boys' at Salisbury.

Now we entered upon the last days of this most remarkable Australian tour, and there were fears that the final moments might lose their significance, for an outbreak of polio was reported from Western Australia. It would have been heartbreaking if the royal visit to Perth had been cancelled, but fortunately the authorities found a way around the difficulties. They asked Her Majesty to submit to a series of strict precautions which included not sleeping on shore at Perth and not shaking hands with anyone presented.

The Queen knew that these rules were laid down in the interests of the children of Western Australia and she immediately agreed.

We who waited for her arrival at Perth saw that, if anything, these difficulties had made the Western Australians more determined than ever to give Her Majesty a most moving send-off from the Commonwealth's shores. The indoor ceremonies were cancelled, but the outdoor ones shone with a new splendour. Who will forget the emotion of the parade of ex-service men and women before the Queen on the superb green sward that Perth has reclaimed from the wide River Swan? As the thousands of old soldiers, led by the South African War veterans, swung by, we seemed to see made

Escorted by Air Vice-Marshal Murdoch, Her Majesty talks to the crew of the 'Canberra'
bomber that competed in the United Kingdom to New Zealand Air Race
At Perth the Queen chats cheerily to patients at the Hollywood Repatriation Hospital
The Duke adds to his learning as he studies a native cat shown to him at the University of Western Australia

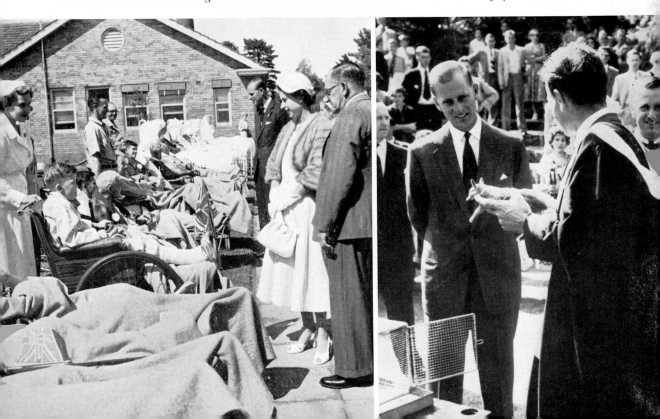

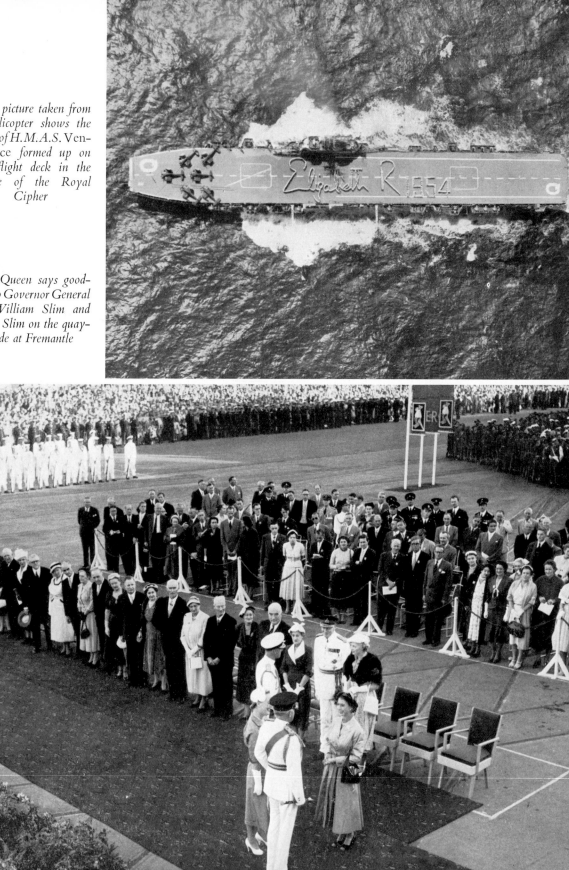

This picture taken from a helicopter shows the crew of H.M.A.S. Vengeance formed up on the flight deck in the shape of the Royal Cipher

The Queen says goodbye to Governor General Sir William Slim and Lady Slim on the quayside at Fremantle

Good-bye Australia, and thank you, we shall never forget. . . .

visible the full extent of Australia's glorious sacrifices in the many wars that she has willingly and unhesitatingly entered side by side with the 'old country' in the common struggle for freedom.

The ball at the University held by the Lord Mayor of Perth could claim to be the most glamorous ball of the whole visit for again the open-air setting brought a new, unexpected splendour to the event. The dancers waltzed under the stars while the towers and mellow arcades of the noble University buildings were reflected in the still waters of the ornamental pool on which banks of flowers seemed to float in clusters of vivid colour. Western Australia has some of the loveliest wild flowers in the world, and the green lawns of the University grounds sloping down to the banks of

the wide River Swan were the perfect setting for a perfect evening.

At last 1st April dawned—the day on which the Queen was to bid farewell to her people of Australia. She drove sadly through the sunshine out of warm-hearted, hospitable Perth to the port of Fremantle.

With ceremony and music she went on board, while the guns thundered their salute and the aircraft of the Royal Australian Air Force roared overhead. She said her last 'good-byes' to her Prime Minister and all the officials who had worked so hard to make the tour the resounding success it was. Slowly the *Gothic* drew away from the quay, leaving so many memories behind—memories of a country and continent which, through the royal visit, had sensed the greatness of its destiny. The tour had revealed to the world the splendour of Australia's achievement and to Australians themselves the opportunities ahead of them for building a noble future. There was pride as well as regret in the cheers that followed the *Gothic* out through the two long arms of the moles that protect Fremantle harbour.

The white ship followed the carpet of gold that seemed to have been laid in her honour over the blue waters by the westering sun. The *Gothic* and her escort of an aircraft carrier and cruisers was outlined against the glowing horizon, and still the thousands watched from the shore and the harbour walls.

Then at six o'clock Her Majesty went to her cabin, to broadcast her farewell message. The radio sets were turned on amongst the waiting crowds on the Fremantle beaches and, with the *Gothic* still in sight, the voice of their Queen seemed to come to them over the darkening waters. Beyond them, all Australia waited and listened, as Her Majesty spoke her last words.

"Our thanks go to you all for your welcome, your hospitality and your loyalty.

And now I say good-bye—God be with you—until the next time I can visit Australia."

Good-bye! Good-bye! Good-bye! Come back again!

Chapter Four

THE JOURNEY HOME

AS the *Gothic* turned north-west from Fremantle on its long journey across the Indian Ocean, there was a 'homeward bound' feeling on board. The major part of the tour was over and had been brilliantly successful, but there was still excitement to come, such as the visit to the Cocos-Keeling Islands.

The *Gothic* stayed for a day, and Her Majesty went ashore to Home Island, where her host was Mr. John Clunies-Ross, to whose family Queen Victoria granted a perpetual lease of the islands.

Then came the enchanting visit to Ceylon. This lovely tropical island as its Prime Minister, Sir John Kotalawala, pointed out, is only as big as Tasmania but yet contains as many people as the whole of Australia. Ceylon received the Queen with all the grace and splendour inherited from its long history of 2,500 years. Her Majesty entered Colombo surrounded by the ancient splendours of the Sinhalese kings. Conch shells were blown

and drums beat a rolling thunder as she took her place in the Freedom Hall to open Parliament the next day. It was a day of moist tropical heat, but Her Majesty looked cool and serene in her lovely Coronation gown, the centre of a memorable scene of gorgeous Eastern colouring.

But indeed the whole of the royal visit to Ceylon was a splendid series of dramatically coloured pictures. Her Majesty and the Duke spent a day, again of fierce overwhelming heat, in the ancient city of Polonnaruwa where modern Ceylon has done a magnificent feat of reclaiming land from the encroaching jungle.

The centre of Ceylon is a country of rugged beauty and high hills, and as the Queen and the Duke drove up the winding road under the triumphal arches and passed the streamers of white paper towards Nuwara Eliya, they were grateful for the cool air that came to them in a consoling stream after the stifling heat of the plains.

Taking the salute from the balcony of Independence Hall in Colombo

High in the hills, they spent a few days of well-deserved rest.

But the climax of the Ceylon visit was undoubtedly the great procession at Kandy where Her Majesty received the rare privilege of being shown the tooth of Buddha, the most precious of all relics to the Buddhists of Ceylon and to the whole of the Buddhist world. Seldom has the Raja Perahera, as the Sinhalese call the traditional procession through the streets to the Temple, been staged with greater brilliance. Through a crowd of over a million people and in the flickering light of torches, one hundred and forty richly caparisoned elephants moved through the streets while the dancers in glittering costumes spun, whirled, and postured before them to the music of trumpets and drums. This was the East in its most opulently splendid mood. It is above all, a memory of intoxicating colour, seen in a land which is yet making rapid progress in Western technology, that the royal party carried away with them as the *Gothic* steamed westward on the final stretch of its voyage as the royal liner.

A glittering Eastern reception greets the Queen on her arrival

For at the rocky fortress colony of Aden on the very tip of Arabia, the Queen and the Duke went ashore from the *Gothic* for the last time. They received a rousing welcome from this small but vitally important link in the Commonwealth scheme of defence.

There were splendid military parades; the Duke visited the great new oil refinery that is being built in Little Aden by over forty thousand workers at a cost of forty-two million pounds; and then, before dawn, the royal travellers took off from the R.A.F. aerodrome on a flight which in a few short hours took them out of Asia into the heart of Africa.

The Queen had now an important task to perform—the opening of the new Owen Falls Dam on the Nile as it leaves Lake Victoria Nyanza.

The political difficulties had somewhat curtailed the programme for the royal visit to Uganda, but they did not detract for one moment from the significance of the scene as Her Majesty stood on the dais to press the button which was to set the Nile running for the first time through the

of the Mediterranean. It bears the proud inscription in Latin: 'An island resolute of purpose remembers resolute men.'

The Queen is no stranger to Malta. She had lived on the island when she was Princess Elizabeth and the Duke had been in command of H.M.S. *Magpie*. The five days of her stay passed all too rapidly. There was a superbly precise military display on the Floriana parade-ground, a state ball in the ancient Palace of the Knights at Valletta, and a flying visit to the little island of Gozo—the first time a reigning sovereign had set foot on its shores.

Gibraltar was the next stop and the Rock looked its proud best, towering up into the bright sunshine, as *Britannia* steamed into the harbour. Her Majesty stepped ashore at Tower Wharf and was immediately presented with the historic keys of Gibraltar, the original great keys of the four gates of the fortress. Again, as befits one of Britain's most ancient and vital strong-points, the emphasis in Gibraltar's welcome was placed on the military parade. Her Majesty reviewed the combined services on the airport runway which stretches from the foot of the Rock to within 500 yards of the Spanish frontier. The Queen afterwards spoke of the future of Gibraltar, urging its inhabitants to 'go forward in the future, in partnership and in amity, for the good government and sure safe keeping of the colony and fortress of Gibraltar.'

The official ceremonies were impressive but there is no doubt at all as to what pleased the royal children most. Prince Charles and Princess Anne were delighted to meet the famous Barbary apes of the Rock, and even more delighted when these most important and exclusive residents condescended to shake hands and to take nuts from them.

Now, westwards and northwards on the last but intensely moving stages of this most important of royal journeys. *Britannia* entered the Channel to be greeted by a wave of popular emotion. In their hundreds the small ships put out to escort the Queen. The guns of the Fleet thundered out their salute, until at last *Britannia* brought her precious freight up the crowded Thames to Tower Bridge and to the wild welcome of London town.

Home Again! Yes, safe in her own house of Buckingham Palace! But surely, Her Majesty was at home wherever she had travelled on her wonderful journey. In very truth, she is now Queen of the Commonwealth.

A number of photographs in this book have been reproduced by courtesy of the HIGH COMMISSIONER FOR NEW ZEALAND *and the* AUSTRALIAN NEWS AND INFORMATION BUREAU